ST IGNATIUS COL PREP LIBRARY

S0-CFL-564

RAVE REVIEWS ☞ **BY DAVID NOONAN.**

"You are reminded of the catastrophe in John O'Hara's first novel, APPOINTMENT IN SAMMARRA . . . Noonan's characters play and drink with the same ritualistic seriousness that John O'Hara's people do." —*The New York Times*

"Funny and sad, balanced between the turmoil of Jim's youth and the soberness of retrospect. The big issues have historical resonance, but it's the smaller stuff—the comic portraits of caddies and golfers, a teenager's search for love and meaning—that Mr. Noonan does best."
  —*Atlanta Journal & Constitution*

"Wildly funny, sad and vivid."
  —*The New York Times Book Review*

"Although covering familiar territory—small-town America and a young man moving from childhood certainties to the ambiguities of adult life—first novelist Noonan writes so well that it's worth the trip."
  —*Kirkus Reviews*

"A cross between CATCHER IN THE RYE and BILLY BATHGATE . . . spiked with sharp dialogue and temperalike descriptions of places and protagonists . . . believable and somberly entertaining."
  —*Booklist*

"More than anything else I wanted to stay right there on the beach forever. Just keep the radios playing and the waves crashing and the sun shining and the gulls swooping overhead, keep it all just like that. Don't change anything, don't go anywhere or do anything or say anything important at all. Don't tell anybody anything. Don't talk about lovers or love affairs or husbands or wives. Don't tell your brother a thing. Just hand him a beer and point out a girl with a nice chest. Don't say a word. . . ."

MEMOIRS OF A CADDY

ST. IGNATIUS COLLEGE PREP
1076 WEST ROOSEVELT ROAD
CHICAGO, ILLINOIS 60608

DAVID NOONAN

ST. MARTIN'S PAPERBACKS

97 — 26 23

NOTE: If you purchased this book without a cover you should be aware that this book is stolen property. It was reported as "unsold and destroyed" to the publisher, and neither the author nor the publisher has received any payment for this "stripped book."

FIC
NOO

This book is a work of fiction. Names, characters, places and incidents are either products of the author's imagination or are used fictitiously. Any resemblance to actual events or locales or persons, living or dead, is entirely coincidental.

Published by arrangement with Simon & Schuster

MEMOIRS OF A CADDY

Copyright © 1991 by David Noonan.

Cover illustration by William Sloan.

All rights reserved. No part of this book may be used or reproduced in any manner whatsoever without written permission except in the case of brief quotations embodied in critical articles or reviews. For information address Simon & Schuster, Simon & Schuster Building, 1230 Avenue of the Americas, New York, NY 10020.

Library of Congress Catalog Card Number: 91-18145

ISBN: 0-312-95059-4

Printed in the United States of America

Simon & Schuster hardcover edition published 1991
St. Martin's Paperbacks edition/May 1993

10 9 8 7 6 5 4 3 2 1

For my sons
David and Raymond

I tramp a perpetual journey.

—WALT WHITMAN
Leaves of Grass

1

I should have known it was going to be a long season when old man Woods dropped dead right in front of me on Easter Sunday morning. He was lining up a putt he wouldn't have made anyway when he slipped to his knees with a grunt and pitched forward. I'd never seen a dead person before, except for people in their coffins, but I knew Woods was dead from the way his face bounced on the grass.

"I'll get Doc Farrell, he's two holes back," I said, and I took off down the center of the fairway as fast as I could go. I was pumping right along when somebody up ahead yelled "Fore!" I couldn't see anything so I bent at the waist, put my hands over my head and kept moving. The ball whistled past my ear, missing me by a foot. As I ran through the group of golfers I saw my buddy Ned. He was standing under a tree lighting a cigarette, the golf bags hanging from his shoulders. "Old man Woods dropped dead,"

I yelled at him. He raised his eyebrows high in acknowledgment.

Doc Farrell was on the seventeenth tee, sitting in a golf cart. "Dr. Farrell," I said, running up to him. "Mr. Woods just collapsed on the eighteenth green. I think he's dead." He gave me a look.

"What makes you think he's dead, son?"

"I don't know," I said, out of breath.

"Get in," he said. I hopped in the cart and we went riding back at top speed. As we came up the eighteenth fairway we could see a small crowd of golfers and caddies gathered on the green. When we got close we saw Woods in the center of the group on his back. His plaid pants were undone, his jacket was thrown open and it looked like his shirt had been torn right up the middle; his bony chest was a cold white against the green of the grass. His head was cocked back, his broken eyeglasses lay nearby, and there was a bit of bloody drool glistening on his cheek. His eyes were closed.

"It looks like your diagnosis was correct," Doc Farrell said as he climbed out of the cart. "Maybe you should think about medical school."

I was standing on the edge of the green with Ned when Mrs. Woods came wailing down the hill from the clubhouse, surrounded by a bunch of lady golfers in pastel skirts and sweaters. Somebody had closed up Woods's jacket and zipped up his pants to make him a little more presentable, but he was still dead and when his wife saw him she screamed and fainted. Now the two of them were sprawled out there on the green and the crowd was growing. There was the sound of a siren in the distance.

"Do you believe this?" I said. Ned looked at me and shook his head.

"It's too weird," he said. "Look at Man o' War."

Man o' War, the other caddy in my loop, was off to the side, pacing back and forth and talking to himself. He was a stooped old black man about sixty-five or so. He didn't look too healthy, but he could walk and walk. He dressed the same every day—white dress shirt buttoned to the neck, black suit pants, and heavy black work shoes. He had gotten hit in the head with a golf ball once, so he wore an old scuffed-up hard hat all the time and he was bald and the hat was big so it sort of rolled around up there. He wasn't a real good caddy—he had a tendency to drop his bags and go off in the woods and take a long shit now and then—and he wasn't very friendly either. In fact, between old man Woods and his buddies and Man o' War, I'd been part of just about the worst loop of the day. Now Woods was dead and Man o' War was acting strange. I walked over to him but he ignored me.

"You all right, War?" I said. It wasn't easy to understand him at any time, since he only had a couple of teeth and was always chewing cigars, but now he was agitated and that made it even harder. His old black face was worry in motion. The only words I could make out were "bad shit," which came out "baasheee . . . baasheee. . ."

The ambulance came and the medics wanted to work on Woods, but Doc Farrell told them it was too late. Mrs. Woods was starting to come around, but when she saw them loading her husband onto the stretcher and covering him up with the blanket she screamed and collapsed again. Doc told them to take Mrs. Woods and send another ambulance for the body. That left old man Woods lying there on the stretcher by the side of the green. Then Ned's foursome and the rest of the golfers had to decide whether to finish playing or not. They stood around talking about it for a while and everybody figured Woods was a sport and he would have wanted them to play out, so they all went back out on the course and picked up where they had left off. Me and Doc Farrell and the other members of Woods's final foursome stayed there with the body. Then Doc decided it would be better if we moved Woods out of the way, so I helped him roll the stretcher down the road. It was heavier than I expected and the little wheels kept twisting, which made it tough to steer. We stuck Woods under a tree near the ninth-hole lake. Ned came over when he was done and we sat there on the grass and had a smoke and waited for the ambulance. It was a cool, sunny day; the pale blue sky said spring, but the bare trees and the black water of the lake were whispering winter. Woods looked like a mummy with the blanket over him.

"Did he say anything before he died?" Ned asked me.

"Nope," I said. "He just dropped and that was it. What do you think it was, Dr. Farrell?"

"I don't know, son. Heart attack maybe, stroke . . ."

"He was putting for par, too," said old man Snyder. Of course, that wasn't quite accurate. Old man Woods had never come close to parring the eighteenth hole, but he had a way of keeping score that made anything possible. And his regular playing partners were the same way—they all cheated on each other. When it came time to mark down the scores on a hole they would all look back down the fairway and concentrate and replay the strokes in their minds and gesture with their fingers, little arcs with their fingers re-creating in miniature the beautiful shots they had made, the rising and falling line of the ball through the sky and down the middle of the fairway. Then, with straight faces, they would say "five" on the par fours and "six" on the par fives. Now and then one of them would really work up his nerve and actually declare that he was putting for par, which is what Woods had done on the last hole of his life. Such cheating was possible because they only saw each other on the tees and on the greens. In between, when they were actually playing the hole, they were spread out all over the place and the only ones who knew their real scores were themselves and their caddies, and their caddies didn't care.

We heard another siren and soon we saw the second ambulance coming down the road.

"I don't think Frank really minds this too much," Snyder said. "He loved this place."

"That's true, Ted," Doc Farrell said. "Maybe you ought to give him that last putt, what do you think?"

"I think that's a great idea, Doc," said Snyder. And with great ceremony old man Snyder took out the scorecard and gave old man Woods a par four. Then he reached down and patted his dead friend on the arm. "Nice putt, partner," he said.

After they took Woods away, Ned and I climbed the hill to the clubhouse. The hill was the best and the worst of the job. It meant you were done, but it was long and steep. I was halfway up when I realized that Woods hadn't paid me before he died.

"Shit," I said, "Woods never paid me."

"Oh, man," Ned said, "you gotta be kiddin'."

"I wish I was."

"That sucks."

"Maybe I should ask Snyder," I said. "He was Woods's partner today."

"Did he pay you yet?"

"Yeah, he slipped it to me when we were coming up the eighteenth, like he always does."

"You could try," Ned said, "but he'd probably give you some shit. The cheap fuck never carries more than six bucks when he plays anyway."

Six bucks was the minimum per bag for eighteen holes that year, but almost everybody was paying seven bucks—everybody but guys like Snyder and Woods, that is.

When we got back to the caddy yard I was surrounded. Everybody wanted the details and they all talked at once.

"Did he puke blood or anything?"

"Did he shit his pants? I heard you shit your pants when you die."

"Was he Catholic? Man, you die on Easter, I'll bet you go straight to heaven, unless you got a mortal sin on your soul."

"Did you hear a shot? Maybe somebody shot him. . . ."

"Nobody shot him, dipshit."

"Maybe they shot him with a poison dart or something. It's possible."

"Were you scared?"

"Did they use those electric things on him, those jumper-cable things? Fuckin' A, I'd love to see that."

"What did it sound like? Did he make any weird sounds?"

"What are you asking me stupid fucking questions for?" I finally said. "You guys saw him."

"Yeah, but he was already dead by then. You saw him before that, when he actually died."

"I was looking the other way."

"Bullshit."

"He just fell, that's all. Like he was kneeling down and then he just tipped over. That was it."

"Fuckin' A, I wish I'd seen that."

"No you don't, asshole."

"Fuck you."

"Did he pay you?"

Of course it was Little Petey the blackjack genius —not to be confused with Pete the Meat, the three-hundred-pound moron—who asked the key question. He'd been out in the woods looking for golf balls and killing birds with his slingshot and had missed most of the excitement, so he was detached enough to get to the point.

"Snyder paid me," I said.

"Right," Little Petey said, "he paid you six stinking bucks all folded up. What about Woods?"

"He never got around to it."

My status changed as I said the words. I went from a guy who saw a guy drop dead, which was cool, to a guy who carried a hacker's bag for eighteen holes and didn't get paid for it, which was not so cool. The joke was on me, and it was a good one.

"You got stiffed by a stiff," said Little Petey.

They laughed, and the phrase passed instantly into the language. "Stiffed by a stiff."

My comeback was no match for Little Petey's eloquence.

"Go fuck yourself," I said, remembering as I said it that it was Easter Sunday.

Then Tommy the ass kisser who worked in the bag room announced that since Woods wouldn't be needing them anymore the contents of his golf bag, everything but the clubs and the bag itself, were now on sale. But Tommy was quickly overpowered, and Woods's balls and tees were stolen on a first-come first-served basis.

Ned and I headed off across the course. My mother was making a ham for dinner.

"Hi, boys," she said as we came in the back door, "did you make a loop?"

"Yup," I said. "What time are we eating?"

"About five. Would you like to eat with us, Ned?" There were eight kids in the family, and my mother thought nothing of setting extra places at the table.

"No, thanks, Mrs. Mooney," Ned said. "We're going to my aunt's house."

"Is Dad home?"

"No, he's down at the town hall. He took Erin and Liz with him."

My father was heavily involved in local politics. He was a member of the board of aldermen, and because it was a small town the aldermen had all kinds of extra jobs. At one time or another he had been the fire commissioner, the housing commissioner, the head of the recreation commission, the head of the board of health, and just about everything else. That year he was serving as the police commissioner.

My sister Noreen, the oldest, was out from the city for the weekend. She was watching TV with Jack and the twins, Maura and Jill.

"You guys get out?" Jack asked. He was ten and anxious to become a caddy.

"Oh yeah," said Ned. "Your brother had a great loop, didn't you, Jim?"

"What happened?" asked Jack.

"Old man Woods dropped dead on the eighteenth green."

"No shit!"

"Watch your mouth, Jack," Noreen said. "What happened, Jim?"

"One of my golfers had a heart attack or something. He died."

"Right on the course?"

"Yeah," Ned said, "and he never paid him either."

"Oh, man," said Jack.

"Stiffed by a stiff," I said.

"You poor thing," said Noreen, "that's a horrible story."

After a while the car pulled into the driveway, the front door opened, the girls went out to the kitchen, and my father came and stood over us as we lay flopped out in front of the television. Jack couldn't wait to tell him.

"Daddy, the man Jim was caddying for dropped dead."

"I heard about it. What happened, pal?"

"It was pretty weird, Dad," I said. "He just fell over. I went and got Doc Farrell, but it was too late."

"He never paid him, either," Jack said.

My father looked at me.

"Doesn't matter," I said.

"That's life," he said. "It's time for dinner. Go wash up."

My mother sat at one end of the table, my father at the other end, and in the middle was an enormous ham surrounded by bowls of mashed potatoes, peas, creamed onions, turnips, rolls, pickles, olives, celery, butter, mustard, everything.

"Let's say grace," my father said.

Saying grace was a part of every dinner, and at big meals, like Easter, we gave it the full-length, enunciated treatment. Slowly and in unison we made the sign of the cross. "In the name of the Father, and of the Son, and of the Holy Ghost, Amen. Bless us O Lord, and these Thy gifts, which we are about to receive, from Thy bounty, through Christ our Lord, Amen. In the name of the Father, and of the Son, and of the Holy Ghost, Amen." Other times, though, especially when my father wasn't around, it was possible to get through the whole thing in seconds. Instead of reaching slowly from head to heart to shoulder to shoulder, the sign of the cross was just the flash of a hand in front of your face, then the words came quickly.

"Namefathersonholyghostamen.

"Blezolor - aneezyegivs - bowdrezeev - dybownee-crizeolor-amen.

"Namefathersonholyghostamen."

As my father rose to slice the ham, the phone rang.

"I'll get it," Jack said, jumping out of his seat, "it might be Matt."

My brother Matt, the second-oldest, had gone to Florida for Easter with some friends from college, and the old man was not happy about it; he had told him not to go, but Matt went anyway.

Jack came back to the table. "It's Mayor Anderson," he said, "it'll just take a minute." My father put down the carving knife and went to the phone, still carrying the big fork.

"I'm sure Matt will call," my mother said, patting Jack's hand. She turned to Erin and Liz.

"Where did you get the buttons, girls?"

"Mayor Anderson gave them to us," Erin said. She was fifteen; Liz was thirteen. Erin's button was an elaborate thing with stars and stripes, a smiling photo of the candidate and the words KENNEDY FOR PRESIDENT. Liz's was smaller and simpler, just white letters on a dark blue background— BOBBY IN '68.

"That jerk Bobby Johnson is going to want it," Liz said, "but he can't have it. He's a Republican anyway."

2

It was a small town with a lot of churches and a long history. George Washington and his troops spent a mean winter there during the Revolutionary War. George set up his headquarters in a mansion near the center of town and the troops camped in the outlying woods and fields. Later on, the campgrounds and the mansion became historical sites and I spent my years as a Boy Scout hiking around and learning about that winter, which supposedly was worse than the winter at Valley Forge, though not as well-known. The main thing I got from it was a sense of the geography of the place, the lay of the land. Washington picked the town because it was well located and defensible; it came to be known as the "Military Capital of the Revolution." It was a hilly town in rolling, hilly country, less than forty miles due west of New York City. There were high, sharp ridges that ran for miles and round, humplike hills. There were long, narrow valleys; short, wide valleys; and deep hollows. The town had been cut out of the tangled, aggressive woods of the Northeast, and there were patches of heavy growth scattered everywhere. There was a skinny, winding river, a few lakes, some ponds and lots of rocky streams and brooks that ran behind houses and under the streets. There were neighborhoods on the tops of hills, neighborhoods on the sides of hills, and neighborhoods at the bottoms of hills. It was a tough town for bike riding. Some of the streets were so steep they were scary; you couldn't ride up them and you didn't want to ride down them, unless you were crazy, which some people were. From the highest hills, looking east on a clear night, you could see the glow of New York City in the distance. It wasn't the skyline; we were too far away for that. It was just this glow, like a giant dome of light. And then you turned around and looked west, and beyond the lights of the houses, as your eyes adjusted, you saw dark hills and stars.

In those days, the town was just beyond the ugly reach of the urban sprawl. If you headed toward New York you'd hit it pretty quick. The highways that ran out from the city passed just a few miles to the north of us, garish American arteries lined with gas stations, diners, bowling alleys, used-car lots, motels, gigantic Chinese restaurants, and every sort of discount outlet. There were even some homes out there, in treeless housing developments separated from the highways by watery ditches; as you rode by you'd see laundry drying in the small backyards, bedsheets and undershirts flapping in the hot winds created by the speeding traffic. It came close; the plastic and grime of the future were spread out in front of us. But behind us were orchards, farms, and fields of grazing horses, and winding roads to take us into that old country.

The golf course where Matt and I caddied, and where my father and uncles had caddied before us, was laid out in a valley just a couple of miles from the center of town. A small, steep hill rose in the middle of the course and the eighteen holes were spread out around it. The clubhouse and pro shop were on top of the hill, arranged around the putting green. Halfway down the side of the hill, midway between the eighteenth green and the clubhouse, there was a swimming pool; the steep road we climbed at the end of each loop ran right by it, and as we trudged past in the summertime we could smell the chlorine and see the members' daughters glistening in their swimsuits. A lot of the caddies walked to work; in the morning they cut through the backyards of the houses that surrounded the course and in across the fairways from all directions and climbed the hill to get to the caddy yard, which was down behind the pro shop; in the late afternoon they headed the other way, out across the course and on into town.

The events I describe here took place during my fifth summer as a caddy. I was seventeen then; Matt was twenty. I had finished my junior year in high school, and I had just two things on my mind—beer, which I could get, and bare tit, which I could not.

Nothing else mattered to me. I studied the blouses of girls like a scientist, registering every curve, every shadow, every fold and crease of cloth, the rise and fall of every breath. I could sense the delicate pressure on buttons and discern the faintest hint of lace. I didn't care if they were large or small, as long as they were there. Discreetly, like the gentleman I was raised to be, I ogled the clad bosoms of checkout girls, waitresses, classmates, and strangers on the bus. I even eyed the women I caddied for, the members' wives as they were always called, whose swings caused their colorful shirts to stretch so tightly across their chests. Worst of all, at least once a day, in French class, I found myself staring at the severely restrained, consecrated to Christ, but nevertheless extremely shapely bust of Sister Mary Thomas.

It was frustrating because I knew some real assholes who were getting bare tit, and more, on a regular basis. The problem was I didn't know how to talk to the sort of girls who would let you take off their bras. And I didn't know what to say to the girls I did know how to talk to, the girls who wouldn't let you take off their bras, to get them to become the sort who would.

It was a conundrum I struggled with. What I didn't understand was that it was only a matter of time, that all I had to do was wait and I would get bare tit and everything that went with it. I'd have it all. Time would bring it to me, in time—ecstasy and heartbreak, out of nowhere, like the weather. "I'm getting sick of this heat wave," I said to Texas Billy in

August as we climbed the long slope of the thirteenth fairway.

"Oh yeah?" he answered. "What you gonna do
about it?"

3

Texas Billy arrived that year in style and a cloud of exhaust a week after Woods died. He rolled up in front of the pro shop in a 1960 Coupe DeVille with expired Florida plates and one tail fin completely gone. Underneath the dirt and the streak of dried vomit on the driver's door, the car was a memory of white. The overloaded trunk was tied shut with a length of plastic clothesline, and the rear end was riding low, just inches off the pavement. Where the missing tail fin was supposed to be, Billy had rigged up a flashlight with red cellophane taped over the lens.

As the golfers on the putting green, now enveloped in gray fumes, stopped and stared in surprise, Billy swung that long door open and climbed out of his car. With his shiny black cowboy shirt, his wraparound shades, and his yellowy-silver hair greased back in a conk, he looked exactly like what he had once claimed to be—Elvis Presley's uncle. "Goddamn," he yelled, stretching his arms to the sky, "I gotta take the piss of my life."

Wayne, the new assistant pro, came scooting out of the pro shop in a fit. "Get that piece of shit out of here now," he said. "Caddies park down below the tennis courts and you all know it."

Billy looked over at us with a grin on his face. "Hey, flytrap," he said, which was the worst thing you could call a caddy, as it implied a slack-jawed stupidity so profound that flies were attracted to your open mouth, "did I hear you call my automobile a piece of shit?"

"Yes, you did," Wayne said, "and you also heard me tell you to get it out of here, now."

"That's what I thought," Billy said as he moved away from the car. "I was going to take a piss, you know," he continued, "but now I think I'll take a crap as well. And maybe if there's a dirty magazine around I'll beat the fucking meat, too. What do you think about that?"

"I think that whoever you think you are, you are definitely not going to be working at this course," Wayne said. Then he turned to us. "Okay, let's some of you help me move this thing out of here."

We just looked at him and slowly disappeared before his eyes, as only real caddies know how to do. This amazing skill was necessary to avoid bad loops and other shit duty, like shagging balls or picking up cigarette butts the day after big parties. One moment we were all there in a group, staring right at him, and the next moment we were halfway down the first fairway or out in the woods or just floating around and around the immediate area, still there, but not there, silent and somehow out of sight, just a step or two ahead, just around the corner, just beyond the soda machine. It took time to learn how to disappear like that, which is why the new guys always got stuck doing the shit. But moving Texas Billy's car without his permission was something even new guys were too smart to do.

"Come on, Dolan," Wayne said to the smallest kid there, "give me a hand here."

"That car's too big to move," Dolan said.

Which was certainly true. Even without Texas Billy's worldly possessions in it, the car must have weighed nearly three tons. It was an American dream of power, thousands of pounds of metal shaped for speed and pleasure and aimed at the moon. It was supposed to look like a rocket ship; if you tipped it on end you could drive it into space. But the way it hunkered down on the blacktop, it was obvious the thing was a rolling slave to gravity. Though others had enjoyed its earlier, healthier years, the machine had found its true owner in Texas Billy. He had invested it with his personality and transformed it from an inanimate object into a living thing. It was his car and his friend, and he was the only man on earth who knew its ways.

"Never mind," Wayne said, "the asshole left the keys in it."

Stunned, we watched as Wayne climbed in and disappeared behind the wheel of Billy's car.

"Jesus Christ, it stinks in here," he said.

He turned the key and the engine barked once and died. A single ball of exhaust appeared at the back of the car. He turned it again and the engine coughed into sputtering life. Wayne nursed her into an unsteady rumble as the air once more filled with fumes.

"Get it out of here, Wayne!" a member hollered from the putting green. "Get it out of here!"

"Shit," Wayne yelled, as the car began to move, "the power steering doesn't work." We trailed along behind as he wrestled the behemoth around the circular drive and started down the hill. As the car picked up speed, Wayne suddenly stuck his head out the window and screamed: "OH MY GOD! THE BRAKES DON'T WORK! THE BRAKES DON'T WORK! OH MY GOD!" Wayne opened the door to jump out, but the car was moving too fast for that. As we ran down the hill behind it, the car drew away quickly. We could see Wayne bouncing up and down in terror as he sped past the trees and phone poles lining the road. His screams grew louder and higher. With a loud "CRACK!" the car went off the road and through an old split-rail fence.

"He's heading for the ninth green!"

"Fuck that, he's heading for the lake!"

"He's gonna hit those people!"

"Look out! Look out!"

"FORE!"

A group of golfers scattered before Wayne as he tore across the ninth green at forty miles an hour, mowing down the pin as he went.

"HELP ME! HELP ME!" he screamed. "I'M GOING TO DIE!"

The next second, Texas Billy's Cadillac was airborne as it shot off a small slope and out over the lake. It was one of the greatest sights I've ever seen; the car hung there in midair and then dropped, with a roar and a splash.

There was a moment of total silence as we watched the car settle into the mud. The water came just up to the windows and we could see it flowing in and filling the front seat. Wayne was slumped against the wheel, knocked out.

"Son of a BITCH!" said Mr. Fowler, one of the golfers who almost got run over. "Get him out of that car, somebody. Hurry up, before he drowns." He looked right at me. "Get him, son."

"Come on," Ned said, pulling me along. "Let's save the asshole. We'll get us some good loops." Wayne had been filling in as temporary caddy master until the regular caddy master got back from Florida and me and Ned were on his shit list, which is why I'd gotten stuck with Woods the week before.

"What the fuck," I said, and in we went.

"Hey, Wayne, wake up. Are you all right?" Wayne's nose was bloodied and he had a nasty red bump on his forehead, but it didn't look as if his neck was broken or anything like that. There was all kinds of shit floating around him inside the car—empty beer cans, empty whiskey bottles, playing cards, crushed cigarette packages, cigar butts, newspapers, some socks, and a couple of old sandwiches. I gave Wayne a shake and splashed a little water in his face. He groaned.

"Hey, Wayne," I said, "can you hear me? You need an ambulance?" The water was belly-deep and ice cold. My balls ached and I could feel the mud sucking around my ankles.

"Ooooohhhh, my head hurts."

"He's okay," Ned yelled to the people on shore.

"I'm not okay, stupid," Wayne said. "Don't tell them I'm okay."

"Who you calling stupid, Wayne?" Ned said. "Fuckin' A, man, we waded out in this shit to help you. What the fuck?"

"You're right," Wayne said. "I'm sorry. Thank you, fellas."

"That's more like it," Ned said. "Shit."

"Wayne," I said, "do you need an ambulance, do you think?" Wayne shook his head as if to clear it.

"Nah, I don't think so." He looked around him. "Damn," he said, slamming the steering wheel, "this fucking thing has no brakes at all. The pedal went right to the floor. Goddamnit, who was that guy? I'm going to kill him." Some ducks swam over and started pecking at the sandwiches.

"That was Texas Billy," Ned said. "He's been caddying here for years. I wouldn't mess with him if I was you, Wayne, he's tough. He's got a bullet in his head."

"I'm sure he does," Wayne said. "I'm sure he does. Help me out of here, boys."

Wayne was sitting on the grass, looking at the ninth green and moaning when Texas Billy came walking down the hill and along the path of destruction.

Without a word, Billy walked past us to the edge of the lake and looked out at his car. Only the roof, the single tail fin, and the trunk, which had popped open, were visible. His possessions were spreading out in an ever-widening slick of old clothing and gas-oline.

"All right, Billy," Mr. Fowler said, "the man's hurt. Let's not have any trouble now."

Billy turned and spoke carefully. "Pardon me, Mr. Fowler, sir," Billy said, "but seeing as somebody stole my car and drove it into the lake, I'd say we already got us some trouble, wouldn't you?"

"Now, Billy . . . "

"Now, shit, Mr. Fowler," Billy said, "I just drove twelve hundred miles, I'm dead tired, and everything I own is floating in that goddamn lake there. Everything. Now how am I supposed to feel about that, goddamnit?"

"I understand, Billy," said Fowler.

Billy waved his hand in disgust and turned away.

Me and Ned and Wayne were starting to shiver pretty good by then and one of the members offered us his golf cart to ride back to the clubhouse. I got behind the wheel, Wayne got in next to me, and Ned hopped on the back, between the bags. Just as I started to drive off, Billy came striding over. He stepped in front of the cart and pointed at Wayne, who looked like he was about to pass out.

"Arnold Palmer gave me that car," Texas Billy said, "and you wrecked it."

"Did Palmer really give it to you?" Ned asked. He'd only heard the story a thousand times.

"Yes, he did," Billy answered. "He gave it to me when I won the Cleveland Open for him in '63."

"But the brakes didn't work," Wayne said. He'd gone from pale white to pale green and was sort of rocking in his seat.

"You got to pump them," said Billy. "But that's not the point. The point is you owe me a car." Billy stepped closer to the cart and leaned in on Wayne. He got real close and whispered. "And you better pay up, 'cause I'm crazy sometimes. You know what I mean? I been shot in the head."

Wayne turned to me. "I feel dizzy," he said, then he leaned out of the cart and threw up.

"I better get him to the clubhouse," I said. Billy stepped aside and I drove away.

Ned's brother Frank drove over with some dry clothes for us and then we went to check on Texas Billy. He had stripped down to his shorts and made a few trips out to his car. He was sitting under a tree, drying off with a towel someone had brought him from the members' locker room. Billy was lean, with big, bony shoulders and knotty muscles. He had a severe caddy tan; his face, neck, and arms were ruddy brown and leathery, but the rest of him was a pale, and bloodless white. The tan line at the back of his neck was especially sharp. He had some interesting scars and a couple of old tattoos, one a fading death's-head and the other a heart pierced with a sword. Scattered on the grass around him were a couple of pairs of shoes, a waterlogged suitcase, and a few other things he had salvaged. The greenkeepers were already working on the ninth green; the car looked like it had always been in the lake.

"Some fucking mess, hey boys?" Billy said, looking up. His hair was still in place and he was still wearing his shades.

"Goddamn, Billy," Ned said, "old Wayne'll never be the same."

"Stupid little shit," Billy said. "Where do they find these guys?"

"He's from Ohio," I said.

"I guess he is," Billy answered.

"I don't mind getting wet, Billy, if you need a hand," Frank said. Frank was a former caddy who had gone on to bigger and better things working in a gas station.

"No, that's okay Frank. I'll let them take care of the rest of it. I got what I need for now."

"Did you lose any money or anything?" asked Ned.

"Hell no, son. I keep that sort of thing on my person at all times. Don't ever get separated from my roll. Or my papers. Only thing was these pictures here. I had 'em in the glove compartment. They ought to dry, though." Spread out on the grass were a half-dozen snapshots. He picked one up, looked at it, and passed it around. It was hard to make out, but it looked like a bunch of people standing around in a field.

"My momma's funeral," Billy said. "I couldn't get back for it, so my brother took these pictures and sent them to me. They mean a lot to me, goddamnit. I ought to wring that little cocksucker's neck."

We drove Billy into town and took his stuff to a laundromat. Me and Ned stayed with the wash while Frank drove Billy to a liquor store. One of the regular drinking spots in town was a wooded hill called Fort Nonsense. The story was that Washington's troops needed something to keep them busy and warm that winter, so George had them construct some earthworks on top of this hill near the center of town. It served no real purpose, so the troops called it Fort Nonsense. It was a park, but it wasn't much of one. It was more like a clearing in the woods, and nobody ever went there except to do things they weren't supposed to do. It was a good place to drink because we could see the cops coming up the road before they could see us and there were plenty of ways to escape.

"Here's to one of the best cars I ever owned. May it rest in peace in Davey Jones's locker." Texas Billy took a slug from a pint of whiskey and chased it with a swallow of beer. The four of us were lined up on a log, with a case of beer at our feet. It was five o'clock, and the early-spring darkness was settling on the hill.

"They said she was unsinkable," Billy went on, "but they were wrong, boys, they were wrong."

"Are you gonna try to get her going again, Billy?"

"No, Ned. She wasn't much longer for this world anyway, I'm afraid. She'll never fly again."

"What are you going to do with her, then?" Ned pressed.

"She's junkyard bound, I guess." Billy looked at Ned. "Unless you want her."

"Well," Ned said, "I been taking auto shop, you know. Maybe I could do something with her."

"Then she's yours, my friend." Billy raised his bottle in a toast. "And may the Phoenix rise again on the wings of your mechanical genius."

I laughed for no reason and the sound echoed in my head. We were drunk.

"I'll tell you one thing," I said, "I've never seen anything like it when that car took off over that lake."

"I wish I'd seen it," said Frank.

"Me too," said Billy, "me too. A Cadillac in flight is a pretty rare sight." We sat there in silence and imagined the thing.

"It's funny, you know," Billy finally said, "I saw my house burn down once."

"Really?"

"I guess it was fifteen years ago. It wasn't my house, of course. I was renting. But I'd been there quite a while. I remember waking up on the couch in the middle of the night, and there were flames in the living room. Hot! Goddamnit, it was hot. And deadly. My boy was staying with me then, and I ran to the stairs and yelled and he came flying down into my arms. He was around twelve then, I think."

"Shit," Ned said.

"We got out all right. Old wooden house on a country road. Firemen came, but it was too late. We stood there and watched it burn, big flames. Me and the boy, wrapped in a blanket. He was crying a little bit. A fireman came over and patted me on the back. Everything going up in smoke—books, pictures, clothes, TV, bills, furniture, the whole fucking thing. And you know what I was thinking? I was thinking, 'Good. Let it burn and good fucking riddance.' No more shit to own. Nothing. I could go anywhere, do anything. Better for everybody. The boy would go back with his mother. I hugged him tight and looked at my car. That's what I did. I stood there and watched my house burn down and thought about driving away in my car, which was safe in the driveway there, with fire hoses running over it. Different car."

Billy took another drink of whiskey and stood up.

"Goddamn," he said, and walked off into the woods. He yelled to us from behind a tree; his voice came out of the dark. "Woke up in Delaware this morning, boys, with a hard-on and a headache."

Ned tipped his head back to finish a beer and fell backward off the log.

"Oh, what did Delaware, boys?" he sang as he lay there on the ground. "What did Delaware?

"I don't know, Alaska, I don't know Alaska.

"She wore a brand New Jersey, that's what Dela wore."

4

On a drizzly Saturday morning in early May I got stuck shagging balls when one of my two golfers, a doctor, got called away for an emergency just as we were about to tee off. His partner decided to get in some practice while we waited for him to return, so the next thing I knew I was standing at the bottom of a long, sloping hill holding a small, empty leather bag. The fifty or so balls it was meant to hold were piled at the feet of the golfer, who was standing at the top of the hill. He waved me into position—I was the target—and took his stance. "Fuck this," I thought to myself as I stood there in my damp sneakers, imagining the crack of the ball against my skull. "I'm too old for this shit."

Shagging balls was the lowest form of employment available on the course, which is why the youngest, least experienced caddies usually got stuck doing it. It was degrading work, running around picking up golf balls, and it was dangerous too. Getting hit in the head with a ball was the worst thing that could happen to a caddy, except for getting struck by lightning, and yet they used to stand us out in that field and hit balls at us over and over again. I could never figure it out. And they wouldn't let you hide behind a tree and wait until they were done, either. You had to pick up the balls as they were hit, to save time. I once heard a member mumbling about how shagging helped the caddies learn to see the ball as it came off the club and follow it through the sky. That was bullshit, though. I was a good caddy, and the only thing I ever learned from shagging was how to duck and what it sounds like when a golf ball just misses your head—it's a mean tearing of the air, a nasty rip right past your ear. All I could think about was taking one in the eye. *Whap! Squish!* Blood on my cheek. Next thing you know I'm a one-eyed fucker with a blind side to worry about. I used to stand out there and close one eye and try to get a feel for it. In sixth grade I read a biography of Louis Braille, and when I shagged I thought about him. I could never shake the image of him playing in his father's workshop and jabbing that awl down into his own eye by accident.

The golfer swung. I heard a click and looked up into the white sky. I saw nothing. The golfer was watching the ball the way golfers do, his club frozen in the air, at the top of his swing, his head tilted. I stood in my spot with my hands on my head, my elbows forward to shield my face, and frantically searched the sky. I grimaced and waited and then there was a thump as the ball landed a few yards to my right. I ran to pick it up. As I grabbed it I heard another click. I looked up quickly and saw the golfer in his pose, staring down in my direction. I froze there, crouched, with my hands over my head again. I knew I looked ridiculous but I didn't care. I was not interested in looking cool while I was shagging. I was not interested in anything to do with shagging. I was interested only in not being knocked unconscious. The ball came down with a *whomp!* ten feet to my left and buried itself in a soft patch of turf. I was digging it out of the mud when I heard the next click. "Goddamnit," I said aloud. I didn't even look up this time, I just knelt there with my hands over my head, waiting. There was another *whomp!*, louder this time, closer, just five feet away. He was zeroing in on me. Then came the click again. I turned my back to the golfer, dropped to one knee, put my hands over my head, and braced myself. "Shit," I thought, "he's got me this time." And that's when I spotted my brother Matt walking alone through a stand of tall trees at the edge of the field. As the ball slammed down beside me I straightened up and trotted toward him. "Hey, Matt," I yelled, "what are you doing here?"

"Jim," he said, reaching out his hand, "Christ, you're still growing." We hadn't seen each other since Christmas. He grinned at me and slapped my shoulder as we shook hands. "Congratulations on that Adam's apple. It suits you." I'd grown from five-six to five-eleven in less than a year, a spurt that saved me from a life as a shrimp and left me with a neck like a sea bird. "Now," said Matt, "step out of the line of fire and let's have a smoke. What are you doing shagging, anyway?"

"Mix-up," I said. "We're waiting for somebody. When did you get home? Have you seen Mom and Dad?"

"Not yet."

Matt was only three years older than me, but we lived in different worlds. He led a complicated life. He was a smart, handsome guy with a knack for fucking up and an easy, charming manner that usually won him the second, third, and fourth chance he needed to fuck up again and again and again. Fifteen years in Catholic schools getting smacked around by nuns, priests, and Christian Brothers who wanted him to conform had left him neither bitter nor dull, as it had so many others. It had merely left him independent, in that he didn't give a fuck about a lot of things that other people worried about all the time, like flunking out of school.

"Is school out already?" I asked, though I knew it was not.

"I'm out," he said, dragging on his cigarette, "out on my ass."

"What happened?"

"Same old story. You don't want to hear. Except this time I duked out the dean, Brother Henry."

"Oh no . . ."

"Oh yeah. They were actually thinking about criminal charges, but I talked them out of it."

"Oh, Matt, what the fuck."

"Anyway, I've decided to forgo my education for now and make a name for myself as the greatest caddy in the history of New Jersey. I've rented a room on Ogden Street, like the true alcoholic I aspire to be, and I have selected my wardrobe for the summer." He stuck his hands in the pockets of his sport jacket and spread his arms wide. "What do you think of 'Seersucker' as a nickname?"

"Are you serious?" Matt had a way of creating impossible situations and then just ignoring the fact that they were impossible. When he was a senior in high school he fell for a pretty girl who just happened to be a novitiate, a nun in training. Horrified at the life she had chosen, Matt convinced himself he was in love with her and set out to save her from the convent. He kissed her at last, under an oak tree, in the fading light of a late fall afternoon. But someone saw them and told what they saw. Such a sin. Matt was expelled and the girl was sent away. He tried to find her, he even called her parents, but they wouldn't tell him anything and he never saw her again.

"I don't think the old man will want to see too much of me this summer," Matt said. "The rooming house is the perfect solution. I'll be in town, I'll see Mom and everybody, but no tension. How's Jack?"

"Jack's fine, they're all fine. But, Matt, what about the draft?"

He shrugged. "Fuck the draft," he said. "If they get me, they get me."

"Yeah," I said, "but what about the war?"

"The fucking war," said Matt. He reached out and picked a piece of grass off my shirt. "I don't know. If I gotta go, I'll go. Fuck it, lots of guys are going."

"Fuck, Matt . . ."

"Hey," Matt said, "what can I say?" He looked past me, over my shoulder. "Who's this fly coming here?"

It was Dolan, carrying an empty shag bag. There were two new golfers taking their stances on the hill; my man was gone.

"What's up, Dolan?" I said.

"I'm shagging for two guests," he said. "Your guy said to pick up the balls and head back." Just then there came the unmistakable sound of a well and powerfully hit drive; the faint but distinctive *whack!* and *whoosh!* carried from the top of the hill.

"Shit," I said, "they're not supposed to hit drivers here." I stepped out away from the trees, waving my arms and yelling and as I did the first drive screamed in over our heads and ricocheted wildly off the trees.

"Motherfucker!" Matt said.

"Get down, Dolan," I said. A second drive tore through the branches above us. I yelled and waved but they ignored me and sent a third rocket in about ten feet off the ground. *Wock!*

"How about these assholes?" Matt said. We were tucked in tight behind the trees. "Come on, let's get the fuck out of here."

"Which way?" Dolan said, as balls continued to crash in around us.

"Right up the middle, boys," said Matt. "We'll charge the fuckers, just like the fucking Light Brigade. You ready?"

"Ready," we said.

So we leapt to our feet and charged with a roar across the field . . . "FUUUCCKKK . . ." and up the hill . . . "YOOOUUU. . . ."

5

We were caddies and we walked everywhere. On weekend mornings we got up before seven and walked through the sleeping town to the golf course, down empty streets, past houses sitting quiet and still in the cool morning shade. We saw signs of life —a doll under a bush, a bicycle on a lawn, a car in a driveway with a forgotten cocktail from the night before poised on its curving roof—but few people. There were still some milkmen left and sometimes we'd see one rattling up a hill in his stubby truck, standing at the steering wheel. Drowsy-looking cops would roll by in their patrol cars, blowing on cardboard cups of coffee, and nod at us. Once we saw a woman in a nightgown sitting on her front porch, her face in her hands, crying. And once we saw a guy sitting in his car in the middle of the street, motor running, sound asleep, while the traffic light above him changed from red to green to yellow to red to green to yellow again and again; it was so quiet you could hear the light click with each change. In the center of town the sunlight slanted in through the tall trees on the green and reflected off the store windows. Alone on the wide sidewalks we studied the oxford shirts, Levi's, and penny loafers it was necessary to wear that year if you weren't a hippie. Then we walked out on Jefferson Avenue, which, as a roadside plaque pointed out, was part of what had once been known as the Continental Highway, another echo of the Colonial days. One of the oldest roads in the East, it wound its way from Wilmington, Delaware, through eastern Pennsylvania, up through New Jersey, and on into New York State. Rendered obsolete as a highway, it had devolved into hundreds of local thoroughfares, its name changing every few miles. One stretch of it was a narrow, two-lane blacktop cut into the side of the long, steep ridge that ran along west of the course. Like a lot of the older roads in town, it was flanked only sporadically by sidewalks of varying lengths and types; slabs of heavy gray slate laid in the nineteenth century gave way to worn dirt paths gave way to strips of crumbling blacktop to worn dirt paths to brand-new concrete with names scratched in it to worn dirt paths. It was lined with old trees whose roots buckled the occasional sidewalks and whose branches met overhead. A mile out, just past the small Catholic hospital where my mother had had her babies, we cut down through a backyard and onto the golf course.

The dew was still heavy at that time of morning, so we stayed out of the rough, keeping to the shorter grass of the fairways, and we walked lightly to keep our feet as dry as possible. Some caddies wore heavy leather shoes and some even wore rubbers until the dew burned off, but most of us wore flimsy sneakers with less than an inch of rubber between the soles and the canvas uppers and we started most days with damp feet.

Sometimes we saw deer on the course in the morning, lost suburban deer, New Jersey deer, of all things, their extraordinary senses tuned not to the ancient frequencies of the forest but to the modern buzz of the greater metropolitan area. We'd see the nervous creatures quivering at the edge of a green, their atoms vibrating, their thick bodies looking too heavy for their skinny, sticklike legs, and then, in a blur, they'd be gone, into the trees. They were tragic animals, pursued by howling packs of insane house pets—Spot and his friends in the throes of blood lust —mowed down by station wagons, blasted by tractor trailers. Their world was shrinking around them —state-park deer begat golf-course deer begat cemetery deer begat backyard deer begat interstate-highway-median deer—and every now and then one of them would dash into the center of town and leap through a plate-glass window in what I imagined to be protest but knew was just blind fear.

We climbed the clubhouse hill and gathered in the caddy yard beneath an ancient oak tree. We sat in the shade on a long wooden bench and smoked cigarettes and threw stones and drank soda at seven-thirty in the morning. On a busy weekend there would be thirty or more of us there, ready to work: me and Matt; Ned; Texas Billy; Man o' War; One Eye

Johnny Johnson; the Shuffler; Pete the Meat; Little Petey; Sonny Boy; Dolan; Red Ryder; the Head; Carolina; Charlie Franklin, who had three kids under the age of three and worked about five jobs; Bob Kent, who was on a free ride at Princeton and read *The New York Times* each morning as he waited to be called; and another twenty or so regulars. The origins of the more interesting names were obvious. One Eye had one eye; he had lost the other one to an errant tee shot. The Head was a fifteen-year-old kid with a big head, in the literal sense of the words; he had an enormous cranium. Carolina came from Carolina. The Shuffler was a high school track star and the fastest man in New Jersey in 1935, the victim of a hit-and-run accident that shattered his legs in 1938; he'd been shuffling for thirty years.

A steep flight of cement stairs led from the caddy yard up to the front of the pro shop and the first tee. Lefty, the caddy master, would round the corner at the top of the stairs and all activity would cease as we looked up at him in silence. He would stand there and look us over and then point down, calling us by name. The names he used were often names he had come up with on his own. They weren't nicknames, because Lefty was the only one who used them; he even made up names for caddies who already had nicknames. Ned's last name was McCormack, so he called him Irish. Matt and me he called Money. Some of the names were opinions: "Come on, Noisy." Some were slurs: "Let's go, Whiskey."

A round of eighteen holes was called a loop and we were loopers. The youngest was thirteen, the oldest—who knows?—maybe sixty, maybe seventy, maybe more. It was hard to tell. Most of us fit into one of four basic categories. There were guys like me and Matt and Ned, high school and college students who caddied every day once school was out. There were professional caddies like Texas Billy, Carolina, and Red Ryder, who caddied in Florida in the winter and came north in the spring. We called them the Florida caddies. There were about six or seven of them, and they were pals of Lefty's, who also spent his winters in Florida. There were also local professionals, like Man o' War, One Eye, and Shuffler, who didn't go to Florida in the winter. And then there were the weekenders, like Charlie Franklin, who worked regular jobs during the week and looped on weekends for extra cash.

Some caddies didn't fit in any of the categories. There were a few members' sons who caddied regularly, but, with the exception of John and Kevin Ryan, brothers who were openly at war with their old man and had nothing but disdain for the country-club life, they were a minority who never really were accepted by the other caddies. And there were drifters who would show up out of nowhere, work awhile if Lefty let them, and then disappear. People would just wash up in a caddy yard because caddies always knew about caddying. If a caddy landed in a strange town and needed money, he'd find the golf course. If he knew the basics and was patient, he'd get a loop. Others showed up not knowing anything except that you got paid in cash as soon as you were done, drinkers looking for drinking money, and these guys had no chance, unless there was a big tournament going on, in which case Lefty would hang bags on a dead man. The weekenders were generally the most serious of the caddies, young husbands and fathers who weren't interested in caddy-yard bullshit, who just wanted to get out, get paid, and get home. For the rest of us, though, the caddy yard was home.

"Your feet are wet again, Jim," said One Eye with disgust. "Why do you boys wear them fucking sneakers?"

"They're comfortable."

"Bullshit. They got no support. You should wear real shoes, golf shoes, like I do."

"He's right," Texas Billy said. "Your feet are the only feet you got, you have to take care of them. I knew a man let his feet rot so bad, they finally had to cut 'em off."

"There you go," said One Eye. "I rest my case."

"A caddy should wear golf shoes," Billy added. "The name of the game is golf."

"Exactly," One Eye said. "Golf is the name of the game, goddamnit."

Cash was the name of the game. That was the best thing about being a caddy. We worked and we got paid, a handful of money. And we needed it, too. In the morning the caddy yard was one big empty pocket. We were flat broke, tapped out. The job did not lend itself to saving. If a kid had a buck and a half as the day began, he was flush and would lend out half of it to those less well off than himself. A soda cost a quarter, so a quarter was a nice piece of money, especially if you didn't have one. A quarter had heft, character, and George Washington on it. It made a nice sound when you dropped it into the

soda machine. We were calm in our morning broke-
ness because we knew there was money up ahead in
the afternoon, and we were extra calm if we had
cigarettes. How sweet the weight of a fresh pack of
smokes in my shirt pocket, with the matches tucked
inside the cellophane wrapper, the complete smoking unit. Smoking was a big deal with us; we did it
with style. Each clean white cigarette was consumed
with flair. First I'd tap it on the face of my watch to
pack the tobacco nice and tight. Then I'd strike a
match without tearing it from the matchbook, using
one hand, take that first deep drag, exhale through
my nose, blow smoke rings, do the French inhale,
study the smoke as it twisted up from the ember,
burn holes in a newspaper, give someone a light rolling the tip of my cigarette against theirs, burn holes
in a leaf, burn an ant to death, put the cigarette out
slow in a puddle of soda, dismantle the butt, ex-
amine the cottony filter turned brown with tar, pull
it apart, toss it away, have another smoke. Only this
time I leave it in my mouth the whole time, hanging
from my lip as I talk around it and squint through
the smoke.

They also sit and wait who only sit and wait and
sit and wait in the cool morning air for Lefty to
beckon. "Come on, Money," he finally said, pointing
right at me. I had just won a breath-holding contest
and nearly blacked out when I stood up.

It was a routine loop and it went well until the
thirteenth hole, when one of my golfers drove his
ball into the edge of the woods on the right. I got up
there ahead of everybody else and found the ball; it
was out of bounds by about two feet. "O.B.," I

shouted back down the fairway. "Hit another." The golfer was supposed to return to the tee and hit another ball but he kept walking toward me.

"Where is it?" he asked as he came through the weeds. He wasn't too happy.

"Right here," I said. "Just out." He stared down at the ball for a minute, then lined it up with the white stakes that marked the course boundaries. "Goddamnit, son," he said, "this ball shouldn't be out." He gave me this weird look and I knew right away what he was talking about: he was pissed off because I hadn't kicked the ball back in bounds.

"I'm sorry, sir, that's where it landed." Fuck it, I wasn't going to cheat for him. I only cheated for the big gamblers, who appreciated it and paid for it. It was understood during certain loops that the caddies would be helping their golfers any and every way possible. Blatant cheating was out, but improving a lie in the rough while "searching" for a ball, kicking a ball a foot or so to keep it in play in the woods, or indicating the line of a putt with your foot as you tended the pin were acceptable tricks. It was a subtle thing that balanced out because everybody involved knew when it was happening and knew the unwritten rules. I would only do it on special occasions, and this was not one of them.

He picked up the ball, trudged back to the tee, and topped his second drive. I had to run down and give him his three wood. I lost interest and the loop was shit from then on; the guy criticized everything I did, and half the time he was right. I expected him to stiff me out of my tip when we finished, but he came through with the seven, which just proved how cheap old man Woods really was.

As I rounded the corner at the top of the caddy yard I heard the sounds of a card game coming from the caddy shack and I felt a little charge of excitement. Blackjack was our game, fast and easy, lots of hands, lots of action. By the time I got to the bottom of the stairs I had a plan. My roll consisted of two fives and four singles, so I'd play with the singles. If I was hot, they'd be enough; if I wasn't, I'd lose them fast and walk away with ten. I put the fives in my wallet and stepped into the caddy shack. It was a dank room of cinder blocks and makeshift wooden tables and it had a kind of pissy smell. What little light there was came from two holes where cinder blocks had been left out to make crude windows. The walls were covered with graffiti and the plywood floor was strewn with racing forms, pages torn from girlie magazines, stray cards from old decks, empty beer and soda cans, cut-up golf balls, and about a million cigarette butts. Every now and then Lefty would get sick of the mess and make some fly sweep the place out.

Little Petey was dealing. I watched a few hands and he was winning, as usual. I thought about starting with fifty-cent bets, but when you win a fifty-cent bet you think, Shit, I should have bet a buck, and that's a loser's thought. I squeezed in next to Cleveland Flowers, a big, tough-looking black man who had changed his name to X the year before. He was a card player and political agitator who quit caddying because it was too much like slave labor. "There won't be any motherfucking golf after the revolution," he used to say. "You can bet your white ass on that." He had his anger and he liked to scare people, but he and I got along okay because my grandmother lived next door to his grandmother.

"Hey, X," I said, "where you been?" It was the first time I'd seen him that season. He was lost in the game and it took him a moment to respond.

"Oh, Jim," he said, when he saw it was me, "how you doing?"

"I'm fine," I said. "You winning?"

"Not yet," he answered. "Not yet."

"You in, Mooney?" It was Little Petey, leaning toward me with the deck in his hands.

"Buck," I said, and dropped a single on the table.

I started well. I won my first two hands and most of the others won with me.

"Come on, Jim," X said, "turn the shit around now."

I bet two dollars and won again. Suddenly I had eighteen bucks. Another two-dollar win and I'd have twenty, a very nice number indeed. So in I go for the two and—bang!—Little Petey deals himself a blackjack. Okay, no problem. I'm still ahead two dollars, so I bet the two, what the fuck, it's not my money. I've got thirteen and he's showing a queen. Hit me, a ten, bust out. Goddamnit, Little Petey's got thirteen too. He hits it and busts out. Should have waited. All right, don't worry. I'm back where I started and I've still got a plan. But I abandon the plan and bet two again. Bang, loser. Shit, supposed to bet one. Goddamnit. Bet another two. Bang, loser. Shit fuck. I've lost four hands in a row to the baby-faced little asshole. The singles are gone. Okay, think. What now?

Two fives in the wallet. He just shuffled, I'm due. No way I lose five hands in a row. If I bet the five and win I'm back to fifteen bucks and if I hit blackjack that's ten dollars and I'm up to twenty. Yes. I feel it, I feel that blackjack. I take out the fives and drop one on the table. Look out, a big bet, a serious bet in that game. And my first card is . . . an ace, oh yes, here we go. My second card is face down. I take the cards in my hands and squeeze real slow. Come on baby, come on blackjack, now's the time. I see it, I see my card, I see my . . . deuce. Fuckin' A! And some fly hits the blackjack, my blackjack, for fifty cents. Get the fuck out of the game, kid. Okay, hit me, Petey, hit my soft thirteen with a most attractive and necessary eight. Fuck, a ten. Now it's a hard thirteen. Nausea coming on. I have to hit it. Come on, baby, give me that eight, give me that no-good fucking eight. Nine—I'm a loser. Five stinking bucks left. Shit shit shit. Okay, no way I lose another hand, no way, so break the last five and bet three bucks and here we go yes here we go yes no yes no yes yes yes. Two queens. Thank God, goddamnit. At last I had a hand, a nice solid twenty. And Little Petey that shit had sixteen. Well, fuck him. X, who had been getting killed with me, was also sitting on twenty. Little Petey looked at us; he knew we had him beat.

"I gotta hit it," he said. Well go right ahead, you little rat, hit it with a sledgehammer.

He turned over a five. "Twenty-one, dealer wins," he said in his squeaky voice as he gathered in our money.

"Motherfucker cocksucker son of a bitch piece of shit no good kiss my fucking ass little bastard," said

X, leaning across the table and shaking his big black fist in Petey's little white face. "If you're cheating I'll cut your fucking throat." Little Petey paid no attention, he just shuffled the cards and dealt again. When he came to X he looked up at him and smiled that shitty little smile. "You in or out, X?"

X took out a twenty and dropped it on the table. "I'm in, you little fucker," he said.

I looked at my pile, I had two dollars left. I'd lost six hands in a row. My head was spinning. I picked up my money, bummed a cigarette, and stepped outside for a moment to think. I was picturing my comeback—two dollars is a dreamer's roll—when Lefty appeared at the top of the stairs. The caddy yard was empty except for me and some sick guy who had wandered away from the V.A. hospital. He just showed up that morning in his pajamas and slippers, with his hospital ID bracelet on his wrist. We figured he was from World War II, he was that age. He shook a little bit, but he was quiet. After a while we started giving him cigarettes and then Matt bought him a pack of his own. He sat there all day at the end of the bench and smoked them.

"Let's go, Money," Lefty said. "I got a good one for you."

"What is it?" I asked. At that time of day the only possible good loop would be the pro and the club champ going out for a few quick holes, or some of the big gamblers leaving the bar to bet on trick shots.

"Nine holes, husband and wife," said Lefty, "let's go." More bullshit, I thought. Nine holes with a husband and wife late on a Saturday afternoon was not good. The husband had played eighteen already and was probably drunk. The wife was most likely one of the dreaded "nine-hole ladies" who usually played on Tuesday mornings, the worst golfers on earth. The game they played wasn't even golf, it was more like polo without horses; they'd take a three wood and knock the ball down the fairway twenty yards at a swing, all the way from the tee to the green. They talked constantly and barely stopped to take a stance. They only played nine holes, and only the front nine. When they finished they would stare in awe at the tenth hole, with its unavoidable tee shot across the water, an insurmountable obstacle that barred them and their formless, flailing style from the back nine forever.

It was a bad loop Lefty had for me, no question, but I was broke so I climbed the stairs. Slowly. A long day was getting longer. And then I came around the corner of the pro shop and saw Mary Butterworth on the practice green, biting her lower lip in concentration as she bent over a fifteen-foot putt. She stroked the ball well and when it dropped into the cup she looked around to see if anyone was watching. There was no one but me.

"Did you see that, Jim?" she called across the green.

"Yes, I did, Mrs. Butterworth," I answered. "Great putt."

"I'm getting better," she said as she walked to the cup. "I'm definitely getting better." I watched her bend down and pick the ball out of the hole.

She wasn't perfect. She was about five feet six, with blond hair, blue eyes, white teeth, straight nose,

long neck, a few freckles on her shoulders and in the
hollow of her throat, high, soft breasts that rode like
two small dreams beneath her white polo shirt, and
long, tan legs with just a little too much muscle at
the calf. She was the only woman golfer I ever knew
who could wear those socks with the pom-poms at
the back and not look dumb. She didn't care who
carried her bag. She was nice to all the caddies, including Man o' War and the Shuffler. "Oh, Shuffler,"
I heard her say one time after she drove her ball into
some high weeds off the sixth fairway, "how do you
put up with me?" Unlike most of the members, she
looked right at you when she asked you a question,
like what club to use, and she always called you by
your name, not "caddy" or "son" the way the others
often did. She had a direct gaze; she looked into
your eyes. When you were with her, you were with
her; she knew who you were, paid attention to what
you said, laughed at your jokes, paid the full seven
bucks, and at the end of a round she thanked you
with a smile that made you want to marry her right
on the spot.

She was twenty-three that summer and so far out
of my reach she might as well have been in another
universe. It wasn't just her age or that she had always been rich or that she was married or that she
was beautiful. (At least I was taller. I hadn't been
when I first caddied for her. I'd been a little kid and
she had actually patted me on the head.) There was
something else keeping us apart—sex. She knew
about it and I didn't. She had a sex life and I didn't. I
was obsessed with it and she wasn't. People who had
sex as a regular part of their lives fascinated me. I

couldn't understand why, if they could have sex whenever they wanted, they bothered doing anything else. Why play golf, of all things, when you could stay home and have sex for four hours instead? It wasn't that I wanted to have sex with Mary Butterworth, though I thought about that often enough. It was more a case of my being constantly aware, when I was in her presence, that she dwelled in the realm of sex—dwelled in it and probably liked it.

I wasn't in love with her at that point. That came later, after everything else happened. In the beginning I was only enthralled by her, a circumstance as hopeless but not nearly so painful as love.

She was married to Sean Butterworth, who had been her boyfriend all through high school, and they were my idea of what being an adult was all about. They weren't too old, they had money to spend, they could drink whenever and whatever they wanted, and they had cool cars. He drove a mean, rumbling GTO that was barely street legal; she drove a white Le Mans convertible that seemed to float as she steered it slowly around the country-club grounds. He was a stockbroker or something in the city. She was a hospital volunteer and a housewife, with a maid.

Sean was two years older than Mary and as wild as she was beautiful. As a teenager he'd been a serious suburban rebel with a talent for cracking up cars and getting into fights that made him a legend by the time he was eighteen and landed him in the Army at twenty-one. On the day in the spring of 1965 when he should have been graduating from some rich kids' college, he was landing instead in a faraway land called Vietnam. He got shot in the chest that fall. The bullet pierced his lung, came out under his right arm, and smashed his elbow. He came home wilder than ever, with a Silver Star, a Purple Heart, and a hitch in his golf swing from the bad elbow.

Sean came out of the clubhouse carrying a bottle of beer, his spikes clicking out the quick rhythm of his walk. "Let's go, baby," he called to Mary. I shouldered their bags and walked ahead of them down to the first tee. Her bag was baby blue and light as a feather; his was what we called a trunk, fat and heavy, made of tooled leather.

"At least we got a good caddy," Sean said. He finished off the beer in one swallow and dropped the empty in a trash can filled with empties. "How are you, Jim?"

"Fine, Mr. Butterworth." It was the first time I'd caddied for him since the fall, and I realized we were almost the same height.

"Quick nine with the wife," he said as he pulled his driver from his bag. Mary heard him as she came up the path.

"Quick nine with the husband," she said, handing me her putter. Sean laughed and grabbed her around the waist. He lifted her off her feet and spun her around.

"She's tough," he said, "she's as tough as they come." He kissed her on the neck and put her down. She took her three wood and stepped up on the tee.

"Dollar a hole, Butterworth," she said. "Can you handle it?"

"How many strokes am I giving you?"

"Three."

"Only three?"

"On each hole." As Sean and I watched in surprise, Mary swung and drove her ball high but straight, a hundred and fifty yards down the middle of the fairway. She waited proudly on the tee for a compliment.

"Nice drive," I said.

"Very nice," said Sean. "I hope mine's that straight."

Sean was a good golfer with a bad temper that kept him from being a great golfer. Great golfers expect to make bad shots now and then and when they do they learn from them and then let them go. Not Sean. He hated bad shots and when he made one he got mad at himself and the world and cursed and threw clubs and talked to himself and got all worked up and then, very often, followed the first bad shot with another just as bad or even worse. The energized calm that golf required, the relaxed tension of it, eluded him. He wanted to kill the ball. He was strong too, a middleweight with broad shoulders and powerful arms, so his mistakes were usually big ones. He hit long, long drives, his favorite shots. When he stood over the ball on the tee, his biceps bulging from the sleeves of his golf shirt, the long muscles in his forearms rippling as he adjusted his grip, he had a small smile on his face; he was going to hit the ball harder than a ball had ever been hit and it was going to go farther than a ball had ever gone. Then he coiled into his backswing and exploded out of it, the long club whipping around in an arc and through the ball. If he liked the shot, the smile turned into a satisfied grin. If he didn't, it became a grimace and a curse.

While Mary seemed at ease in the world—her walk was smooth and she even knew how to stand with her hands at her sides and still look natural—Sean was the opposite. He was restless, wired up, always in motion. His walk was a charge and he simply couldn't stand still, not even when he was waiting for another golfer to hit the ball. It used to drive his playing partners crazy, the way he'd hop around all the time, herky-jerky, as though there was heat coming off the earth or something, as though the ground was too hot to stand in one spot for more than a second. There was too much energy coursing through him and he had to let it off with constant toe tapping, head bobbing, finger snapping, all these little movements, quietly dumping energy; he had to let it off or it would back up and overload and he'd blow like a high-voltage transformer.

He was a little drunk that afternoon, so his swing was relaxed and his shots, though shorter than usual, were straight. The first few holes went smoothly. I forgot about the blackjack game and began to enjoy myself. Mary was sweet, as always, and Sean was friendlier than he'd ever been. The course was empty and in the late-afternoon light the fairways, the greens, the rough, and the trees, all different shades of green, looked soft and rich. Along the edge of the woods the shadows deepened into darkness, as though night was gathering there.

It was genuine peace and quiet, for a while. On the fourth tee Sean even danced; he did an impression of Mary's mother doing the chicken-back at a wedding. He hopped around like a screwball, and the more Mary laughed the harder he hopped. Then, as we approached the fourth green, Sean froze.

"Look there," he said. A gopher was sitting just off the back of the green, silhouetted against a toolshed.

"That must be the gopher Joe Lacey has been complaining about all month," whispered Sean. "He's a brazen little bastard, isn't he?" Sean touched my arm and I put his bag down. Mary was on the other side of the fairway. Sean quietly searched through the bag and came out with a gun, a big black .45. What the fuck? No wonder his bag was so heavy. He moved me aside and, bracing himself on the golf bag, took aim at the gopher.

Mary looked over at the last second, saw Sean in his stance, and screamed.

"Sean, no!"

Sean fired. The big gun jumped in his hands and the gopher exploded.

"Got him!" he said.

"Goddamn you, Sean," Mary shouted. She started to cry. "Goddamn you." She threw down her club and started toward us, then turned and walked off in the direction of the clubhouse. Sean started after her, but stopped.

"Mary," he yelled, "Mary, wait, please, I'm sorry. Mary, please, it was only a gopher. It was tearing up the greens. I'm sorry. Mary." She never looked back.

"Ah, shit," Sean said.

As we inspected the gore, Sean explained what a lucky shot he had made. "It was really at the limit of what the weapon can do, Jim. To tell you the truth, I'm surprised I hit the little fucker."

"Why do you carry a gun in your golf bag, Mr. Butterworth?" I think he was surprised by the directness of the question because he gave me this look like he was actually seeing me, which was not a look you got too often when you caddied. Then he smiled at me.

"Well, Jim," he said, "I guess it's just a habit, you know?" He kicked a piece of gopher off the green, grabbed his driver, and headed for the fifth tee.

We finished out the nine holes and Sean played good golf. He putted better than I'd ever seen him putt before. He seemed to forget that Mary had ever been with us. Then, as we came down the ninth fairway, he mentioned her.

"I fucked up, Jim," he said. "You saw it. Not the first time, not the last time."

"It happens, I guess."

"Yes it does, Jim, it does." I could see that he was thinking hard and complicated thoughts. "I love my wife," he said after a moment. I let that one hang there in the dusk. We kept walking and then Sean laughed. Suddenly I knew what he was thinking.

"Asshole gopher," I said. Sean laughed again and slapped me on the back.

"Dead asshole gopher," he said. He paid me twenty-five bucks for the nine holes and asked me to caddy for him the next morning.

6

Matt's rooming house was a big, white Victorian place with a set of rickety wooden stairs nailed to the front of it. The stairs, which were technically a fire escape, zigzagged down from an attic window to the front lawn. They were made of raw, weathered lumber, and if there was ever a fire it was a sure bet they'd burn fast and hot. "A wooden fire escape is a pretty interesting idea," Matt said when he first moved in. "I wonder who thought of it." The stairs were as ugly as they were flammable; they destroyed the wedding-cake lines of the ornate old house and gave it a deranged look. The landlady, Mrs. Henry, hovered constantly in the front hall and challenged all who entered. "Who's that?" she yelled when she heard the doorknob turn. "Oh, it's you," she said when she recognized the person. There were ten rooms available, on a weekly basis. Texas Billy and Red Ryder had rooms on the second floor. Matt was up in the attic, which had been divided into four tiny garrets. The ceiling in his room slanted sharply—the only place he could stand full height was just inside the door—and the floorboards were full of splinters. There was a tired old bed, a straight-back chair, a beat-up bureau, and an iron standing lamp with a yellowed parchment shade. The best thing about the room was the fire escape, which was just outside the window and served as Matt's porch. We sat out there quite a lot that summer. The view wasn't much, just people passing on the sidewalk, walking dogs, riding bikes, getting in and out of cars, going in and out of houses, but it had a certain lazy rhythm that was easy to fall into, and of course on clear nights there were stars.

I was hurrying to tell Matt about Sean Butterworth and the gopher when I spotted him out on the fire escape. It was just getting dark. He was drinking a beer and trying to read by the light coming from his window, holding the book close to his face. He was a serious reader and I could see that he was deep into the book, oblivious of his surroundings. I stood on the lawn a moment and watched him. You could tell just by looking at him that he was intelligent; that's what drove my parents crazy. He had a good brain but he wouldn't apply it to school work except in total emergency situations, when he'd consume half a year's worth of material in a weekend. He was brilliant but unmotivated, his teachers had always agreed, and when they scanned his future from their hard little seats at the front of the room they saw nothing but unhappiness awaiting him. I thought they judged him harshly and I found their predictions, which they made over and over again in notes to my parents, cruel and simple. How could such inherently boring people dare to declare my brother a failure? I myself was of the salt-mine school of scholarship; I climbed down into the pit every day and worked hard with strictly average results. I "applied myself" to the great mountain of disconnected facts they threw up in front of us in a manner that satisfied exactly the low expectations of the petty tyrants who ran the institutions. I was their dream student, neither too dumb nor too smart to require any special attention. I was perfectly mediocre in the classroom; they didn't have to think about me at all. The system fit me like an old suit, so of course I knew the real reason Matt's teachers had doomed him to a life of struggle and disappointment: He would never be one of them. He had imagination and they didn't. He saw a world they couldn't see. He couldn't see it too well himself, maybe, but he felt it instinctively, and it excited him. He knew it was a world that had nothing to do with school or grades or being elected president of the student body. I don't think he knew much more than that, really, only enough to reject convention and leave himself open to experience, only enough to get himself in trouble. I sometimes wonder if he knew how dangerous a world it was, if he was frightened by it, or by his need to live in it. If he was, it never showed.

"What's the book?" I asked. Matt was climbing through the window as I came through the door.

"The *Bhagavad Gita*," he answered. He tossed it to me. "You want a beer?"

"Sure." He had a six-pack on ice in a wastebasket.

He flopped on the bed as I sat in the chair and flipped through the book.

"What's it about?"

"Everything. Some people think it's the greatest book ever written."

"No shit."

"Oh yeah."

The beer was ice-cold; the breeze coming through the window was cool and sweet and carried the rich smell of spring into the room. I could hear the soft rush of the trees and see their new leaves waving around the streetlights. I was hanging out with my brother on a Saturday night. I had money in my pocket, a story to tell, and some crazy book in my hand: "I am come as Time, the waster of the peoples, ready for that hour that ripens to their ruin." I even knew about a party some girl was having. The possibilities were limitless.

"You hungry?" Matt asked.

"Starving."

"You want to go to the diner?" Matt was definitely into the professional-caddy lifestyle.

"Why don't we eat at the house," I suggested. Our parents lived less than a mile away. "There's lots of stuff in the refrigerator."

"Is the old man home?"

"I'm pretty sure he's got a meeting. It's just Mom and the kids."

"Let's check it out."

My parents were more pissed at Matt than they had ever been. My father had shut him out completely; when Matt tried to explain what happened at school, he walked out of the room. He wasn't inter-

ested in any more explanations, he said, and he
didn't want to hear any bullshit about caddying and
rooming houses. He was beyond disappointed, he
was disgusted. "I've had enough, Matt," he said, "just
stay out of my sight." My mother was angry too, but
she was also worried. She was afraid Matt was going
to wind up in Vietnam. Of course the old man was
worried about that as well, but he never came out
and said it because that wasn't his style. The pattern
that evolved was for Matt to come by the house once
or twice a week when my father was out. He'd eat
something, fool around with the little kids for a
while, and then my mother would sit him down and
try to talk some sense into him.

I told Matt about the gopher as we walked. He
didn't like Sean Butterworth, he never had, and he
was happy to hear that Mary had walked away.
"Good for her," he said. He wanted to know exactly
what they said to each other and how they said it.

"I don't know why she married that asshole," he
said. "She's so fine, and he's so nowhere."

"He ain't that bad," I said. "He's just a little crazy."

"Carrying a gun in your golf bag is not a little
crazy, Jim," said Matt. "It's real crazy."

"I guess the war did it to him."

"Fuck that, he was nuts before the war. I remember the time he smashed his car into that wall on
Route 24 and practically cut his fucking head off.
The cop had to hold his neck together with his bare
hands to keep him from bleeding to death. Two
weeks later he's out on the putting green, joking
about it and showing off his two hundred stitches."

It was one of the town's famous automobile accidents, of which there had been several over the years. The details changed, but the basic story was always the same. The formula included high speeds, teenagers, alcohol, missed turns, telephone poles, big old trees by the side of the road, yearbook photos of the dead in the newspaper the next day, and, in the spring, a sad graduation ceremony. RIP, Most Likely to Succeed. It was true suburban carnage, the Grim Reaper in a Dodge Charger, and almost tradition. After each crash there were pilgrimages to the scene of the accident and visits to the gas station where the crushed, bloodstained vehicle was left on display as a warning to others. That Sean Butterworth was still alive when he was pulled from his own inevitable wreckage was actually a function of his craziness; cops from three towns were chasing him when he went off the road at ninety miles an hour.

"It's too bad he got shot over there," Matt said, "but he's an arrogant bastard and that's all there is to it."

"Well," I said, "all I know is, he's teeing off at seven-thirty tomorrow and he wants me to carry his bag."

"Who's he playing with?"

"Goodman and a couple of guests. They're good and they're fast. We'll be in by eleven. Which means two loops easy, maybe more. If you want, I'm sure Lefty will put us out together."

"I don't know."

"Come on, Matt," I said. "You and me. Who cares about the golfers?"

"Maybe," he said. "Let me think about it." The fact

was, Matt didn't need my help to get an early loop. He had entered into a period of nonstop looping, and Lefty was taking full advantage of it. It was a thing most caddies went through at least once or twice a season, when they stopped fooling around and got down to serious money-making. Normally, the job was pretty relaxed. You got there when you got there, made your loop, and then either played cards or drifted back into town. You only took a second loop or an extra nine holes if you felt like it, and a lot of the time you didn't feel like it. But then a time would come when you suddenly needed to make some real money, to get ahead, so you'd go into one of these streaks where you made as many loops as you could until you dropped. You went to Lefty and told him you'd be coming early and staying late, and he liked that because there were always late loops or bad loops that nobody wanted. So he'd get you out first thing every morning and then you'd be there for him when he needed you. It was a real burnout—forty-five holes on Saturday, forty-five holes on Sunday, twenty-seven on Tuesday and Thursday, thirty-six on Wednesday and Friday. It required concentration, focus, and no distractions—no card games, no goofing off in the caddy yard. You were now a super looper, willing to walk from dawn right into the dark of night carrying any old bag, and the other caddies recognized it and respected it. It was possible, with minimal spending, to bank a hundred and fifty dollars or more a week during these runs, but you could only keep it up for two or three weeks at the most before simple exhaustion forced you back into the normal routine. I usually made my move in the late summer, with school looming and the new style rules coming into focus. Even a five-and-a-half-hour death march with Judge Norman and his cadaverous cronies was bearable if it meant I was halfway to owning those sharp new ankle boots, the ones that looked just like the ones the Byrds wore on the cover of their latest album. Matt wasn't working for fashion though, he was working to live. He was on his own and had to pay his way in the world.

We were eating cold chicken and macaroni salad at the kitchen table, which was actually a picnic table my father had improved with a Formica top and padded benches, when my mother came in and sat across from Matt.

"How's the chicken, boys?"

"Great, Mom. Thanks."

She watched us eat for a few moments. She was studying us, as she sometimes did, as though she were remembering every day of our lives, just looking at us, her sons, babies once and now nearly full grown, emptying her refrigerator yet again. She reached out and tucked a piece of my hair behind my ear.

"You need a haircut, Jim," she said absently.

"I know."

"Did you loop today?"

"Yeah, twenty-seven holes."

"That's good. How about you, Matt?"

"Two loops today, Mom."

"You're not playing cards, are you, boys?"

"No, Mom," I said. "Not really."

"You know I don't like that."

"We know."

"How's your room, Matt? Do you need anything for it? A rug or anything?"

"I'm all set, Mom. Thanks."

It was all perfunctory; she was working up to something. I could see Matt starting to squirm. She saw it, too, and got to the point.

"Matt, do you have a copy of your transcripts anywhere?"

"What transcripts, Mom?"

"Your college transcripts. You know, the courses you've taken, the marks you've received, your credits."

"Mom, I've been to three schools in three years," said Matt. "I've taken leaves of absence, incompletes, pass-fails. I've changed majors about five times. I've been on probation, I've been suspended, I've dropped out, and I've been expelled. My transcript, if there is such a thing, is not going to do me any good. I'm sorry, Mom, but my college career is over."

The plain truth of his statement made her angry. "I don't like your attitude, Matt," she said. "I want you to put together a list of all the courses you have completed and whatever credits you've earned."

"You're wasting your time," Matt said. "No school's going to take me."

"Just do it, Matt." She got up from the table and walked out of the room. Matt stared down at his plate and shook his head slowly, then looked up at me. The kitchen was suddenly too bright and too empty with just the two of us there. I went out on the back porch for a smoke, which was strictly taboo. As my eyes adjusted to the dark I could make out the swing set at the bottom of the yard and the twins' toys scattered about. Jack had dumped his bike in front of the garage, in the same spot Matt and I used to dump ours. How careless we were, with our bikes and our baseball mitts and our basketballs, how thoughtlessly we dropped them here and there, anywhere, as though they meant nothing to us. My mother was going to find Matt a college that would take him and she was going to put him in it and that was that. He would not be drafted and he would not go to the war. She wouldn't let him. Period.

Matt owned a 1961 Rambler, but one of his college roommates had borrowed it to drive home to Ohio. He was supposed to turn right around and come back but he was a month behind schedule, so we had to hitchhike to the party, which was a few miles west of town.

One of our rides that night was with Bob Hill, a weekend caddy who was taking his family out for ice cream when he picked us up. He was driving a worn-out Ford station wagon full of scrawny kids with dirty faces. I don't know why he stopped for us; there wasn't much room. Bob and his wife were in the front seat with a couple of small children between them and there were five more kids in the backseat.

"Hello, boys," Bob said as we climbed in. Three of the kids scrambled into the rear of the car to make room for us. I'd never seen Bob anywhere but the caddy yard and I had no idea he had such a big family. I could see right away that life was a struggle for them; the kids all had choppy kitchen haircuts and their clothes didn't seem to fit right. Sitting next to me was a girl of about ten wearing a plaid dress a couple of sizes too big. Next to her was a boy of about eight in a T-shirt that squeezed his bony chest like an elastic bandage. There was all kinds of junk on the floor of the car—broken toys, candy wrappers, soda bottles. Bob was forty or so. His regular job was on a loading dock somewhere; one of his favorite caddy-yard subjects was the incredible weight of the things he loaded on and off trucks.

"Marie, these are the Mooney boys, Matt and Jim," Bob said. "They're Alderman Mooney's sons." Bob's wife was a skinny woman with small, dark circles under her eyes. She wore a sleeveless blouse and had a limp ribbon tied in her hair. She smiled at us but didn't say anything. The kids stared. Bob swigged from a can of beer.

"Where you heading, boys?" he asked.

"Armory Hills," Matt said. "How about yourself?"

"Just out for a drive," he said. "I guess we can run you over to Armory Hills." We could sense right away that Bob's family was less than excited about a ten-mile detour. So could Bob, and he shot his wife an angry look. Keeping her eyes on the road, she lit a long cigarette.

"Hey, Bob, you don't have to do that," said Matt.

"I insist."

"No, really," said Matt. "It's not necessary. Anyway, we're meeting some guys out by Harley Road." Matt chose a spot just a mile ahead for the fictitious rendezvous. Good move. Unfortunately, to get there we had to pass the Dairy Queen, the Hill family's original destination. As we drove by the busy ice-cream emporium, the girl sitting next to me couldn't contain herself.

"Oh no," she cried. "There's the Dairy Queen. Stop, Daddy. Stop!"

Quick as a lizard's tongue, Bob Hill's right arm lashed out and he cracked the girl across the face with the back of his hand. Her head jerked sideways with the force of the blow; I could see the red welt forming on her cheek as her eyes filled with tears. She was in shock. Even worse, she was too frightened to cry. She put one hand to her cheek, the other over her mouth, and held her breath.

"That's it," said Bob, "no ice cream tonight." His children received this heartless pronouncement in grim silence; they obviously knew better than to protest. There was nauseating fear in the car; I could feel it. I was afraid myself. I think even Bob was afraid. He tried to joke with us.

"See what happens when you don't wear a rubber, boys?"

Marie reached back and handed her daughter a crumpled tissue, but said nothing. We rode the rest of the way in awful silence.

"What a fucking creep," Matt said as we watched the station wagon drive away. "Someone ought to kick his ass."

"I feel sorry for those kids," I said.

"You ain't kidding. Poor little bastards."

"He works hard, though," I said. "I mean, it doesn't make sense. Why would a guy knock himself out to feed his kids, then turn around and beat them?"

"Nothing makes sense," said Matt, "except that nothing makes sense."

Armory Hills was a development of big neocolonial houses set on half-acre lots that were carefully carved out of the surrounding woods. It was the high end of tract housing, right there on the border between middle class and upper-middle class. The people who lived in the neighborhood weren't rich, they were well-off, which meant they could handle a big mortgage, two or three car payments, private-school tuitions, and, in some cases, a country-club membership and still have something left over to tip the bag boy at the grocery store. But they had to keep working or the whole thing would fall apart, and fast. The men were all executives of one kind or another. Some were taking part in a regional boom and drove to work at the office complexes and industrial parks that were springing up everywhere. Others took the train into the city every morning. The homes all had five bedrooms, four bathrooms, finished basements, two-car garages and big front lawns with huge boulders and tall, original-growth trees worked into the landscape. Out back there were redwood decks and sloping yards bordered by thick woods that were part of a county park. The residents, even the kids, liked to point out the fact that the parkland could never be developed. This pleased them, for obvious reasons, but Matt said they were subconsciously glad more people like themselves would not be moving there.

The development was just a few years old and, in spite of the fact that it was as well designed and built as those places ever were, it had a raw feel to it. The lawns were soft and tenuous underfoot. The shrubbery was too short, the sidewalks too new, the trees lining the streets too skinny, the driveways too black and smooth, the streets too wide and too perfectly curved. The Belgian-block curbstones were preternaturally clean, as though someone scrubbed them every morning, and they met the street too neatly. The door knockers, carriage lamps, and other brass ornaments that adorned the houses were all too shiny. Having grown up in a sixty-year-old house that was basically a block of granite lined with mahogany, I was intrigued by places like Armory Hills, where intercoms and built-in vacuuming systems were standard features. It was like going to the World's Fair.

The girl having the party went to Blessed Virgin, an all-girl Catholic high school that was famous for having more than its share of beautiful blondes, and she was one of them. I didn't know her—she was a junior like me, but as I understood it, she only went out with college football players—but that didn't matter because it was an open party. It hadn't started that way, but the word had spread from school to school and before she knew it her intimate, parents-out-of-town makeout session had become the blowout of the year.

Matt and I got dropped off at the entrance to the development and walked from there. I didn't have an exact address, so we had to wander around for a while, watching for cars and listening for music. Because the driveways were so large, nobody parked on the streets; they were wide and empty and walking them was strange. It was like walking through a ghost town, a perfectly maintained ghost town with all the modern conveniences.

A few years earlier, when life was simpler, all I had to do to find a party was follow the smell of Jade East, the exotic drugstore cologne my friends and I all wore when we were in the eighth grade. It was powerful stuff; when a dozen fourteen-year-old boys soaked themselves in it and squeezed into a basement together, the sweet, chemical stench spread through the neighborhood like an invisible cloud of poison gas. As I neared the source of the reek I'd hear the tinny sound of the Rolling Stones' "Satisfaction" coming through the cheap speakers of a portable record player turned up full. I'd check myself in the side mirror of a parked car—my gray plastic industrial-strength fadeaway-style eyeglasses would be hip in twenty years—and then join my gawky classmates in yet another wood-paneled rec room where, ravaged by puberty and loaded on soda, we'd stomp the night away, driven into a frenzy by that simple, irresistible beat.

We found the party in a cul-de-sac jammed with people and cars. Mixed in with the usual collection of family station wagons and three-hundred-dollar smokers I noticed a couple of genuine rich-kid toys —an orange Plymouth Road Runner and dark blue Oldsmobile 442. The two overpowered sex machines were parked side by side under a street lamp. The owners, surrounded by admirers, stood guard over their vehicles. They couldn't go in the house, for fear something might happen to the cars and they couldn't even lean on them or the rivets in their jeans would leave scratches. So they just stood there and looked at the things and talked about them and eventually got in them and drove away.

We entered the house through the open garage door. The place was packed with sweaty people, from the basement, where the music was blasting, to the top floor, where the bedrooms were in heavy use. There was competitive drinking in the kitchen and foreplay in the darkened living room, where necking couples sprawled on the furniture and across the floor. In the backyard, some jocks had discovered a rope swing and were engaged in a loud demonstration of their simian prowess. The side of the house had become a combination pissoir-vomitorium. The front yard was for quiet drinking and conversation, provided you could find someone to talk to and had something to say. Ideally, I'd meet a girl in the basement, get her out to the front lawn for a chat and then ease her into the living room for an anatomical census.

It took me half an hour to case the joint. It was mostly private-school kids, though I did see a couple of football players from my school in the crowd. By the time I got back to the garage Matt was busy putting his best moves on a half-drunk redhead with the top three buttons of her blouse conveniently undone. They were dancing, and every now and then Matt would lean in and say something and she'd laugh and he'd laugh. Matt was a great dancer; he'd gone to school in Philadelphia for a while and picked up a very smooth Philly style, a loose, finger-snapping slide step that looked effortless and cool but took work to master. There were a lot of details, but the real key to it was keeping your head cocked at a certain angle, chin up, and moving back and forth just so, with the proper air of amused detachment, like a hip king surveying his hip kingdom and digging it, but not too much. I was pretty good at it myself. What eluded me were the quips, the little jokes I was supposed to whisper in my partner's ear. Once I got past "What's your name?" and "What school do you go to?" I was lost.

I was standing there next to the hot-water heater, working up the nerve to ask someone to dance, when Kevin Ryan materialized out of the crowd. "Money!" he shouted when he saw me. "Old man Woods is looking for you. He wants to pay you the six bucks he owes you." He threw his arm around my shoulders. "He really looks like shit, though, I gotta tell ya." He handed me a flask. "Here you go, man. Have a drink. Matt here?" I took a slug of warm scotch, not my favorite drink.

"Yeah, he's over there," I gasped. "Where's John?"

"He's around here somewhere." I closed my eyes and took another sip from the flask. Awful shit. Kevin noticed my reaction.

"Hey, man," he said, "we got a case out in the car if you want a beer."

"Sounds good," I said.

"Well, good," said Kevin, "let's get to it." The scotch was bubbling like acid at the back of my throat. I needed a drink of water.

"You go ahead. I'll meet you there."

"You got it, brother."

I was at the kitchen sink when I noticed this huge guy, a football player, no doubt, standing with his fists clenched, breathing heavily and mumbling to himself. His shirt was soaked with sweat and his face was bright red. He was apparently very drunk and very upset. Some of his friends were trying to talk to him, but he was oblivious. Suddenly this extraordinary girl appeared and consulted with the worried friends. Then she tried to talk to the crazy brute.

"Todd, it's me, Elizabeth. Elizabeth Brooks. Can you hear me?" It was our hostess, a genuine American princess in a denim miniskirt and a white blouse. She wore her hair long and parted in the middle. She had pushed it back behind her ears and I could see two tiny diamond earrings glittering there. She looked intelligent, which surprised me, and, at the moment, grave beyond her years. This was no vacant cheerleader, not that I had anything against vacant cheerleaders. I was close enough to hear her voice, which was soft and had just a trace of the South in it.

"Todd, are you okay?" Todd was definitely not okay. He took a clumsy step away from the girl, in my direction, and groaned. I wanted to get as far away from Todd and his demons as possible but I couldn't take my eyes off Elizabeth.

"Did you take something, Todd? Did you take a pill?" Oh shit, was Todd on LSD? I'd never seen anyone on LSD before. Was this what they called a bad trip, a bummer? Good Lord, it looked like his head was going to explode. Todd shuffled a few more steps to the side and stopped in front of the sink. He gripped the edge of the counter then slammed his head down on it, gashing his forehead right between his eyes. Elizabeth screamed, and one of the guys grabbed Todd from behind. Todd shook him off, reared back, and slammed his fist through the window over the sink. I saw his forearm open up from the wrist to the elbow. As he pulled it back, a sheet of blood gushed from the long, deep wound. A girl next to me gagged and ran from the room. The big dummy stood there in shock, staring down at his arm as his blood splashed into the sink. Another girl screamed. Todd's knees sagged. The fight had gone out of him. He had opened his radial artery; he was bleeding to death.

For five years, from age eleven to age sixteen, I had been a serious Boy Scout. I was so serious, in fact, that I became an Eagle Scout, the highest rank possible, an accomplishment I was very proud of at fifteen and mortified by at sixteen. My success as a Boy Scout was a direct result of my failure as a baseball player. I was fleeing a disastrous Little League career when I discovered the Boy Scouts and I quickly learned that the system, while physical in many ways, readily rewarded the dogged sort of book work that was my specialty. There was a lot of reading and memorization involved and I flew through the ranks. By the time I was done I had mastered all sorts of useless esoterica. I knew how to start a fire in the rain with no matches. I knew which roots, berries, and grasses were okay to eat. And I knew how to construct a rope bridge strong enough to hold a 250-pound man. Ridiculous skills, certainly, but I also knew first aid. I not only knew it but had performed it regularly during summer camp, when my fellow scouts hacked themselves up with remarkable nonchalance. They chopped their feet with axes, sliced open their hands with hunting knives, broke arms and legs falling out of trees, burned themselves over campfires, and knocked their teeth out running through the woods in the dark. Like woodsmoke, spilled blood was everywhere, an essential part of the Boy Scout experience; the stuff had never bothered me.

I grabbed a dish towel off the counter and pressed it to Todd's arm. "You'd better call an ambulance," I said to Elizabeth. She turned to one of Todd's friends. "Call an ambulance, Mark." I raised the arm above Todd's head. "Lie down on the floor, Todd," I said. He didn't hear me but he was ready to go anyway so I eased him down in a kind of controlled collapse. His face was pale; the dish towel was soaked with blood. "We need more towels," I said, "and a blanket." Without a word, Elizabeth went off to get them.

I covered him with the blanket and applied a fresh towel to the wound. I had one of the jocks help me hold the arm closed and another one apply pressure to Todd's armpit. Elizabeth was kneeling beside me, staring, transfixed. "Why don't you talk to him," I said. Todd seemed to be a long way off. As she told him over and over in her lovely voice that everything would be fine, he soaked through three more towels. Finally, the bleeding was under control. We sat there in a pool of blood and waited for the ambulance.

"What's the blanket for?" Elizabeth asked.

"Shock," I said. "To keep him warm." God, she was beautiful. It was a struggle not to look at her chest. She smiled at me.

"You know what you're doing, don't you?"

"I guess so."

"Is he going to be okay?"

"I think so."

Matt pushed through the crowd. "Jesus, Jim," he said as he crouched across from me. "What happened?"

"He punched out the window," I said. "There's an ambulance on the way." Matt studied the mess for a moment, then reached out and patted me on the shoulder.

The ambulance came and the cops came with it. They busted a few guys for drinking and chased everybody else away. In the confusion, I lost track of Elizabeth; we'd met, we'd talked, and she didn't even know my name. I cleaned myself up in the basement bathroom and then Matt and I left with the Ryan brothers.

"Simply amazing," Kevin said as he drove. He raised his beer. "A toast. To Dr. James Mooney, party surgeon."

"What a great way to meet chicks," said his brother John.

"What are you talking about?"

"Hey, man," he said, "I saw you talking to Elizabeth Brooks. She's one of the finest pieces of ass in the known universe. And she digs you."

"She what?"

"She digs you, man. She likes you. She was looking at you, man. You're a fucking hero."

"Bullshit."

"I don't know, Jim," said Matt. "John's got a point. You were pretty cool, and she was right there next to you. She saw what you did."

"No way," I said.

"You should call her, man," said John. "Ask her out."

"You think so?"

"Definitely."

"Really?"

"Absolutely."

I sat back and took a long drink of beer. The car was racing through the dark, trees flashing past. I couldn't wait to look up her number in the phone book.

They dropped us off in front of the rooming house; I was too excited to go home. We were standing there on the sidewalk when Texas Billy came walking unsteadily up the street. He was drunk and happy to see us.

"Hello, boys, hello. What are you up to on such a beautiful night?"

"Not much, Billy. How about you?"

"The usual. Would you care to join me for a nightcap?"

We tiptoed up the wide, carpeted steps to the second floor. Billy's room was much larger than Matt's and he kept it much neater than I had expected. It had a big old iron bed in the middle of it, a rug, lace curtains, a fat armchair, a dresser with a mirror attached, and a small table and chair. His brush, comb, and nail clippers were carefully laid out on top of the dresser along with a few stacks of change. The pictures of his mother's funeral were stuck around the mirror as was a snapshot of a girl in a cap and gown. I didn't see a picture of his son anywhere.

Billy took a bottle of whiskey and some glasses out of the dresser. "Mrs. Henry, as you know, does not allow drinking on the premises, so we must be discreet." It was a hopeful and hopeless rule, since Mrs. Henry rented almost exclusively to drinkers. Billy poured big drinks and passed them out. He looked closely at my shirt. "I know dried blood when I see it, Jim," he said. "Have you been fightin'?" We told him the story, and for once Texas Billy listened without interrupting.

"He's lucky you were there," he said when we finished. "Let me tell you. I've seen a lot of men bleed to death, and it can happen fast. Hell, it almost happened to me once." He freshened his drink, stood up, and took off his shirt. He was weaving just the slightest little bit. "Look here," he said. He stepped closer to the lamp and tipped the shade back. The yellow light fell across his right shoulder. Just below his collarbone there was a lumpy scar about two inches long. Texas Billy outlined it with his finger. "It was on some shitty little island in the Pacific. We had to clean out the last few Japs, see, before we could move on to the next shitty little island and do the same thing." Billy went into a crouch and started creeping around the room holding an invisible rifle. "I was crawling around in a big hole, some kind of coral formation, filled with busted-up palm trees, no footing or anything. I was falling around in there, ya know, when—*bang!*" Billy froze. "This fucking Jap rises right up from under my feet, just like that, rises right up and jabs me with his bayonet. Right here." He pointed to the scar. "I didn't even feel it, I was so scared. I shot the son of a bitch about six times and climbed out of that fucking hole as fast as I could go. I was hotfooting it back to our camp when some Marine sees me and pulls me to the ground. 'You're bleeding, Marine,' he says to me. I look down and my shirt is soaked, my pants are soaked. What the fuck. Turned out the Jap nicked an artery. I was walking along dying and didn't even know it."

Texas Billy sat down on the bed and took a long sip from his drink. When he spoke again he was somber.

"I been close a few times, boys, but that was the closest, let me tell ya. I laid back to wait for the medic and all of a sudden I knew it was over, I knew it was the end. I was a dead man, on my way to join all the rest of the dead. Everything opened up around me and there was a whooshing in my chest, like I was gonna be carried off. Then I started falling backward, down and down, deeper and deeper, darker and darker."

He polished off his drink.

"I was scared, boys. I was terrified. And alone? Lord, I never felt so all alone."

Billy got up to pour himself another.

"You did that boy right, Jim."

I heard the bedsprings squeak. I was in the armchair, Matt was leaning against the wall. I took a sip of whiskey and closed my eyes. I tried to get a picture of Elizabeth Brooks in my head but all I could see was that bloody arm and those dish towels.

I woke up at dawn. There was a blanket over me and my feet were up on the desk chair. Billy was snoring beneath his covers.

7

Sunday morning, which used to mean church, was beginning to mean hangovers. I crept down the hall to the bathroom. The door was locked. I could hear water running and retching sounds. I was suddenly dizzy and sat down on the floor with my back to the wall and my knees pulled up to my chest. The bathroom door opened and Red Ryder appeared in his underwear. He was smoking a cigarette; his head was soaking wet.

"Top of the morning," he said.

"Morning, Red."

Red Ryder was smaller and older than Texas Billy. He had been a professional boxer back in the late thirties and early forties, his main claim to fame a fifteen-round loss to Beau Jack in 1941, just a year before Beau won the lightweight title for the first time. "I put him on his ass in the twelfth," he used to explain, "but I couldn't finish him off, not Beau Jack.

So forget about it, Red, understand? I hit him hard, though. Yes, I did. You better believe it." Red, whose real name was Lincoln Ryder, carried a copy of his page from *The Ring* record book folded up in his wallet. "I had a hundred fights," he'd say, "and I can prove it." But he didn't have to; his nose, flat and pulpy, was proof enough.

Red was all bones in his baggy boxer shorts and T-shirt; he looked like a very old little kid. He gave me a wide, toothless smile; his teeth were still in his room.

"I feel lucky today, boy. How about you?"

"I feel like shit," I said as I stood up. Red started to laugh, but his laugh turned into a hacking cough. He bent at the waist and put out a hand to steady himself on the wall. His face turned purple as he continued to cough; it sounded like he was bringing up chunks of his lungs. As the mess broke loose in his chest, he tottered back into the bathroom, spit it into the toilet and flushed it away.

"Better wake up Billy," he said as he headed back down the hall, his cigarette still burning in his fingers. "Time's awasting."

A few minutes later I learned that Texas Billy liked sardines for breakfast. "Have one," he said, sitting up in bed and holding out the can, "they're good for you." I grabbed my shoes and bolted from his room.

Matt was dressed and lying on his bed, reading.

"Texas Billy's eating sardines," I said.

"They're good for you," Matt answered. He closed the book and sat up. He flashed me his broadest grin. "I feel lucky today, boy. How about you?"

Lefty, who picked up Texas Billy and Red Ryder

on his way to the course each morning, grunted and agreed to give me and Matt a lift as well. He was halfway through his first cigar of the day; the smoke swirled round our heads as we climbed into the car. The great big copper-colored Chrysler, which Lefty drove from Florida to New Jersey and back again every year, was outfitted with every automobile doo-dad on the market—drink holders that hooked on the doors, dangling deodorizers shaped like pinup girls, coin holders, tissue dispensers, little wastebas-kets, a dashboard-mounted compass, a full-length rearview mirror that stretched across the top of the windshield from one side of the car to the other, a suicide knob on the steering wheel, and a tiny oscil-lating fan that plugged into the cigarette lighter. The man knew how to travel by car. There was even a little statue of Jesus Christ, though as far as I knew Lefty prayed only at the racetrack.

We stopped at a red light in front of one of the old stone churches near the center of town. Billy, Red, and Lefty were arguing about a horse; Matt was reading. A handful of sleepy-looking worshippers were arriving early for the seven o'clock service. As I watched, a mother crouched in front of her little girl and cleaned her face with a handkerchief, wetting it with the tip of her tongue and dabbing at the girl's cheek. The walk leading to the church was shaded by an elm and lined with yellow flowers. A splash of morning sunlight played on the wall, just below a stained-glass window. I'd spent a lot of Sundays in church, as altar boy, choirboy, and cutup. I peaked as a good Catholic in fifth grade, during my confir-mation. I was kneeling at the altar in my bright red robe, waiting for the bishop to come along and slap my cheek. I was ready to become a soldier in the army of Christ, ready to go and die battling communists in China. I was expecting something extraordinary from the sacrament, a filling-up of some kind that would change me forever, that would make me tough and holy at the same time, like the priests who went to Africa to save the natives' souls and wound up getting eaten by cannibals. Saving souls seemed like a cool thing to do and I wanted to do it. Then the bishop got to me. I closed my eyes and waited. He tapped me lightly on the jaw and mumbled something in Latin. Nothing. Lightning did not strike. The moment passed. I waited for days for the Holy Ghost to descend upon me, but it never happened. If he was looking for me, he never found me. I was disappointed; they built up the soldier thing a lot. My flame burned lower and lower. By the time I got to seventh grade, I was drinking altar wine in the sacristy after serving mass; a year later my Sundays were devoted to looping. The little girl must have felt me looking at her. She turned in my direction and gave me the kind of dead stare kids give to strangers. The light turned green and as we pulled away she stuck her tongue out at me and made a face. Her mother saw this and yanked her around and into the church.

Matt and I were down the first fairway, waiting for Sean and the others to tee off, when the church bells in town tolled the hour. The sound floated faintly over the valley. Seven A.M., my earliest loop ever. The dew was heavy and when we reached the first green, which was slightly elevated, I looked back down the fairway. We had left footprints, dark green in the pale green of the dew, and I could see the winding trace of play: dark patches where shots were taken, the six sets of footprints—two caddies, four players.

Sean was friendly enough, but not surprisingly we were no longer the intimate pals we'd been the day before. It was business as usual, which was fine with me. They were good golfers; we were good caddies; the loop was fast and easy. Matt tended the pin on the fourth green, which left me free to start down the fifth fairway. When I looked back I could see Sean acting out the gopher murder. He took aim; he pulled the trigger; he showed his friends the spot where the animal had landed. He pointed toward me, the direction Mary had taken when she left. They were all laughing, except for Matt.

"What an incredible asshole," Matt said, as he joined me. "He scares the shit out of his wife and thinks it's funny. So do his asshole buddies." Sean was playing with Randy Goodman and two guests. They were all about the same age, country-club kids who grew up signing for Cokes and fries at the pool; now they signed for martinis and steak sandwiches at the grill. They were cocky and content with their lot in life. Except for Sean's trip to the war, an aberration of his own making, things were working out for them as planned. They had wives; they had jobs; they had low handicaps. As it turned out, some of them even had girlfriends.

We made it to the ninth hole by eight-thirty; the halfway house wasn't even open yet. We'd be finished as early as ten, no later than ten-thirty. I'd make two loops easy and Matt had a shot at the very rare three-loop day—fifty-four holes, a super-looper feat that was beyond me and most of the other caddies as well.

"You could make three today, Matt. Do you realize that?" We were sitting on the tenth tee, waiting for Sean, who had run up to the clubhouse for sodas.

"So could you," he said.

"No fucking way. Two is my limit. You never made three before, did you?"

"No," he said, "three would be a first. I may need a fresh shirt, though. This one's almost gone." Matt's faded yellow golf shirt, which he alternated with a couple of newer ones, was in its second and final year of service. It had several small tears on the right shoulder that were on the verge of linking up.

Caddying was tough on clothes. Pants wore out on the outside of the thigh, where the bags rubbed the seam. Shirts wore out at the shoulder, where the weight of the bags was carried. The younger caddies wore jeans, while a lot of the older guys wore baggy work pants, which were uncool. Shorts were not allowed, no matter how hot it got. Most of us wore T-shirts or golf shirts except for Man o' War, who went with dress shirts, and Texas Billy, who preferred cowboy shirts, some with the sleeves cut off. Some of the weekend caddies wore uniform shirts from their regular jobs with their names stitched on them. Because the work was so hard on clothes, we tended to wear the same stuff over and over until it wore out. Everybody looked familiar, even from a distance. There's Ned over on the eighth fairway, in his trusty red golf shirt. And there's Pete the Meat, strolling down the fifteenth, his belly hanging out of his classic white Fruit of the Loom V-neck.

Sean came down the hill from the clubhouse cradling six cans of soda against his chest. It was the cheap supermarket swill that Lefty sold out of the Pepsi machine in the caddy yard. Sean was impressed by Lefty's audacity.

"The son of a bitch is using Pepsi's machine to sell discount soda," he said as he passed the drinks around. "I wonder how he gets away with it."

"He puts the real soda in the machine before the Pepsi guy shows up, then he takes it out when he leaves," I explained. I'd seen Lefty in his weekly battles with the Pepsi man. "He's had the same five cases of good soda piled up in the bag room since the season began. He stashes the cheap stuff down in the garage, behind the golf carts."

"What does he tell the guy?"

"He tells him we don't like soda."

"Caddies don't like soda?"

"That's right, and when the guy sees these cheap cans everywhere and starts hollering, Lefty says we bring it with us from home. Then, when the guy keeps squawking, Lefty tells him . . ."

". . . he's going to get a Coke machine," Sean finished.

"You got it."

"In-fucking-credible."

The tenth hole was a par three with a carry of about a hundred and sixty yards over water. It was one of those tricky holes that played differently every day. The green stuck out into the lake so there was water on three sides and the back side was lined with deep sand traps; there was no room for error.

"What do you think, Matt?" Goodman had a bad habit of asking his caddy what club to use and then ignoring his suggestion.

"I don't like the breeze," Matt answered. "Hit the six iron, easy six."

"Too much club," Goodman said. "I'll hit the seven."

"Whatever," Matt said.

Goodman's ball was high and straight at the pin, a perfect seven iron. It came down with a splash a foot short of dry land.

"That's wet," Matt said.

"I know it's wet," Goodman snapped. "Are you happy?"

"Am I what?" Matt replied. Goodman seemed to realize he had said something stupid.

"Never mind," he said. Randy was one of those big, soft guys with tits, the kind who sweat gravy.

"Hey, Randy," Matt said, "this may come as a surprise to you, but I really don't give a shit one way or the other." Oh yeah, this was the Matt who got tossed out of school all the time; no respect for authority and not afraid to show it. Randy was insulted.

"You should call me Mr. Goodman." Sean laughed out loud at that one. Matt couldn't believe what he was hearing.

"Mr. Goodman?" said Matt. "Mr. Goodman? You've got to be kidding. You're only three years older than me, Randy. I've known you since you were sixteen. I call your old man Mr. Goodman, not you."

"Come on, Randy," said Sean, "cut the shit and hit another ball."

"He should, though," Randy whined. "He should call us mister. We're members and he's a caddy. That's how it works."

"What the fuck are you talking about?" Sean said. "That's Matt Mooney. This is his brother Jim. They're no different than you are. Wake up, will you?"

Randy hit a second ball, using his six iron, and put it on the green with the others. We crossed the long, narrow bridge that led across the lake from the tee to the green in single file. Randy, just like a kid, turned as he walked and apologized to Matt, who was walking behind him. "I'm sorry, Matt. I just hate going in the water."

"Don't worry about it, Randy," Matt answered. "I'm sure the next generation of caddies will call you Mr. Goodman." Matt laughed, and Randy, not quite sure what the joke was, laughed with him.

On the twelfth hole, a wide, sloping dogleg on the side of a hill, Matt and I found ourselves working opposite sides of the fairway. I was on the high side and I watched him from a distance as he walked along below me, by himself. Head slightly bowed, arms extended to balance the bags, he presented the classic caddy profile as he led the way to the green. His golfers trailed behind him, talking to each other, as Matt walked out ahead of them, alone. That's what I noticed about him, that he was alone. One of the things about coming from a big family is, you're never alone and you never think of yourself as being alone and you never think of anybody else in the family as being alone. They are part of the family and you think of them in relation to the family, or to members of the family. Matt and Jack, me and Jack, Matt and my parents, my parents and me, Matt and me, Matt and the twins, the twins and Jack, Jack and the girls, Matt and the girls, the girls and Noreen, Noreen and Matt. It was never just Matt by himself and certainly never me by myself. We were all linked up, jammed into the same house for years and years, sharing clothes, sharing food, sharing the toothpaste. We were all one, a family, a house full of people, a crowded house, people talking all the time, the phone ringing all the time, people coming and going, no one ever alone, ever, no peace, no quiet, no privacy. Everybody knew everything about everyone else, or almost. Late at night, lying in bed, I'd hear my parents in their room, talking about us—this problem in school, that problem in school, this lingering chest cold, that new pair of shoes. The endless details of our entwined lives held them and us together. Same bathroom, same kitchen, same living room, same basement, same yard, forever. I couldn't imagine not going up that same street every night to that same house. Winter, spring, summer, fall, and winter again, year after year. The only thing that changed was the station wagon in the driveway; every few years we'd trade in an old Chevy for a new Chevy. And every couple of years we'd have a picture taken for my father to use in his campaigns. He'd print up flyers with his record in office and the latest family portrait and distribute them to the voters.

What a beautiful family, everybody said, what a lovely family. And we were, too, all together there, looking out at the world as one, the boys in jackets and ties, the girls in their best dresses, the proud parents, one on each side, enclosing and protecting their children. It was a powerful picture. I see myself lodged in the image, embedded there, like a stone in a wall. All of us stones in a wall, solid, enduring, one. It was in my head that way and I couldn't get it out, couldn't change it. I was part of a family, we were all part of a family, and that was that. Even when Noreen moved to New York, it wasn't as if she had really gone anywhere. She called all the time and came out almost every weekend and brought her friends from the city with her. My mother was always making stuff for her apartment and my parents talked about her all the time as if she were still living with us. And she was, too, in a room of her own (at last) that just happened to be forty miles away. But it was different with Matt, it felt different, and as I watched him that morning, walking out ahead, alone, I tried to imagine what he was thinking. He was living in a rooming house and working as a caddy, and that was cool, that was good. My parents were pissed at him; that was bad. But summer was coming on, and that was good. Walking down the twelfth fairway on a sunny Sunday morning, a beautiful day and money up ahead, was very good, definitely. But something else was happening. What was that? His future? Yes, the big, blurry thing out in front of him, he was walking into it right before my eyes, with golf bags on his shoulders, walking right into it, alone like that, making it happen to him, the draft and maybe the war too. He was walking the same golf course he had walked for years, doing the same silly kid's job, but it was goodbye to being a kid and goodbye to his old life with all of us. His rooming-house rebellion wasn't like his other rebellions, I realized, it wasn't about Matt and my parents, it was just about Matt. It was real; he wasn't fooling around. He was breaking away, from all of us, from everything, and it was strange and scary to see.

We were on the fourteenth green. Matt was tending the pin. Sean was crouched behind his ball, lining up a twenty-foot putt for birdie. I was just behind Sean, looking over his shoulder, trying to read the break of the green. Randy, like the true jerk he was, broke Sean's concentration.

"How's that situation in New York?" Randy said. Sean shot him a hard look.

"Under control," he said.

"What did I hear, something about a scene in a restaurant or something?" Sean stood up.

"Who told you about that?"

"Somebody mentioned it."

"Oh yeah? Somebody who?"

"Somebody, I don't know. What happened? She flipped?"

Sean bent over his putt.

"You're a nosy bastard, Randy. You know that? You always have been. You should mind your own business." Sean putted, the ball rolled four feet past the cup.

"Come on, Sean," Randy said, "I'm your friend, for chrissakes. You can talk to me." Sean, following his ball, stopped in front of him. Randy, an inch taller and sixty pounds heavier, took a step back.

"What do you want to know, Randy?"

"Hey, shit, it's no big deal," said Randy. "If you don't want to talk about it . . ."

"No, really. What do you want to know?" Suddenly, Sean seemed threatening. Randy was frightened, ready to drop.

"I don't want to know anything. Forget it."

"What?"

"Come on, Sean." No one moved.

"You want to know what happened in the restaurant?"

"It's none of my business."

"We had a fight." Randy, in spite of his fear, was interested.

"Yeah?"

"Yeah. A real fight. You know what I mean, Randy?"

"A real fight? Like, screaming?"

"Like, worse."

"You hit her?"

"I hit her, she hit me. It was charming."

"Jesus, Sean. That's bad. Maybe you should end it."

"What do you think the fight was about, you dumb fuck?"

Sean walked off the green, backhanding his putt as he went. The ball rolled all the way across the green and down into a sand trap. I started after it, but Sean stopped me. "Fuck it, Jim," he said, "leave it there." He went over to the next tee, sat on a bench, and lit a cigarette. The others whispered as they putted out.

"He's been seeing this girl in the city."

"Does Mary know?"

"No, I don't think so."

"And now the chick's freaking out?"

"Sounds like it."

"Who is she?"

"A waitress, in the Village. You know, an actress."

"Hippie-dippie."

"Yeah, I guess."

"That's what happens when you get involved. One night only, two nights at the most, then bye-bye baby. No matter what. The other thing is suicide, guaranteed."

When they were finished, Randy took out the scorecard. "Okay, let's see. That's par for me and . . ." He looked back in the direction of the sand trap where Sean's ball had landed, a smirk on his face. ". . . we'll give Sean a bogie. Hey, we win the hole."

"I fucking don't believe it," Matt said as we headed down the next fairway to wait for the tee shots. "He's got a girlfriend in New York. And he beats her up. In public. What the fuck?"

I had heard about such things, other members, older men, sometimes made vague references while they played, but I'd never ever been privy to such gory detail. I was having trouble understanding the thing, it was on a scale I was not familiar with. Matt was angry.

"I can't believe this," he said. "He's married to her and he fools around? It doesn't make sense. She's fucking beautiful. I mean, she's there in the house, waiting for him, making his fucking dinner, and he's hanging out with some waitress in the city? I don't get it." The tee shots sailed down the fairway. Matt paid no attention. "If she was my wife, I'd be sitting at that table every night, right on time, guaranteed. Hell, I'd get home early. I'd sit there in the kitchen, have a beer, and just watch her cook. Read the paper, shoot the breeze a little bit. That's how you do it. Then you hit the sack."

I had heard Matt fantasize about many things, but never about the simple joys of suburban married life. Although his version sounded good to me ("Time for bed, Jim." "Okay, Mary."), I knew instinctively that there was more to it than food and sex. Of course, I was bothered by the idea that Sean was cheating on Mary, but on the other hand it was the kind of sex weirdness I assumed was part of being married, so it didn't bother me too much, which was kind of interesting in itself.

"I don't know, Matt," I said. "It must be pretty complicated, you know, between them."

"What the fuck are you talking about?"

"I don't know," I said. "Married guys do that kind of stuff, right? That's what they do."

"Where'd you get that bullshit? *Playboy* magazine? The guy's an asshole, Jim. Period." The funny thing was, I did get that bullshit from *Playboy* magazine; when you got right down to it, I believed in free love.

"I believe in free love," I said. "Don't you?" Matt laughed and punched me on the arm.

"I'll bet you believe in free love, you fucking knuckle-knob." We started down the fairway, bags on our shoulders. Matt, trailing me, grabbed the bottom of one of my bags and lifted it. It was an old caddy trick; the clubs spilled out on the ground in front of me.

"See you on the green, guru," said Matt. He flashed me the peace sign as he walked away.

Sean and Mary lived in a big white house behind the sixteenth green. The house sat on a rise, at the top of a wide, sloping lawn that ran down to the golf course. There was a deck on the back of the house and Mary was there that morning, sitting in the sun, drinking coffee and reading the paper. She came to the railing and waved to us as we arrived on the green. They must have worked out the gopher thing.

"How's it going?" she hollered.

"Your husband's winning all the money," Randy yelled back.

"Good, I need it. How's Joanne?"

"Sound asleep, I'm sure. She's bringing the baby to the club later."

"What fun. I'll see her there." She was wearing a white T-shirt and her hair seemed to be pinned up or something, as if she had just gotten out of bed. Jesus. I was thinking about that when she noticed me.

"Morning, Jim," she called, waving. I waved back.

"Morning, Mrs. Butterworth."

"I'll be right back," Sean said, and trotted off toward his house. He stopped below the deck and looked up. Mary leaned over the railing and they spoke. It was nearly twenty feet from the deck to the lawn, which fell away abruptly from the back of the house, and Sean looked small standing there. He must have said something funny because Mary suddenly laughed and reached down in his direction. His raised his arm, as if to take her hand, though the distance between them was too great. They stayed like that a second, reaching for each other, then Sean turned and started back down the lawn.

Mary had always lived on the golf course; her father's house overlooked the fifteenth fairway. She was born to the life—blond and beautiful in upper-middle-class America—and grew up in a big American house with a big American lawn, big American cars in the driveway, a big American dog jumping around on the lawn, and big American trees to shade her from the summer sun. It wasn't the world of the debutante; it was more low-keyed than that. But, like a debutante, she was what the whole thing was all about. The houses and the lawns existed for her; she was the best thing her world had to offer, the best thing in that world, the perfect thing, the beautiful blond daughter. There weren't any coming-out balls; there didn't have to be. It was all very casual. She simply dwelled in her perfect world and grew more beautiful in it every day. She simply existed in her setting. She went to private school in her uniform, played tennis and golf at the country club, went to the dances and the splash parties. There was no need for a debutante ball, because every day was her day, every evening and every night belonged to her. All those lawns and fairways, all that groomed grass, so soft underfoot, so green, so fresh, all those rolling acres spread out around her and set her off, like a jewel in velvet. She was the jewel, an American princess. And if her teenage prince got drunk and tore up the big lawn with his car, or grew up, pulled a gun from his golf bag, and blasted a gopher to bits on the fourth green, well, maybe it wasn't such a perfect world after all, but it was still pretty perfect, wasn't it?

I figured that going out with Sean had been Mary's way of rebelling when she was younger. She felt pressure, I guess, and pulled against it and fell for the bad boy in the group. It was her way of changing the world she lived in without leaving it. If she had been born a few years later she might have become a hippie. But she came just before that time, when the road to rebellion was more personal. You had to do it on your own in the early sixties, within the confines of the world you knew. When the hippie thing came along, it was a ready-made alternative world; you could just wander off into it. It was easy. It was much more complicated to rebel in the prehippie years. You didn't do it as part of a group, you did it by yourself. That's what Mary must have done when she hooked up with Sean.

"She's the greatest," Randy said when Sean returned.

"Fuck off, Randy," said Sean. "Play golf."

We finished before ten-thirty, as expected, and Sean and his partner each gave me ten bucks. "See you next Saturday," Sean said as he paid me; I was now his regular caddy. Lefty sent Matt back out immediately, but I didn't get my second loop until noon. It was four hackers and Pete the Meat and by the time we got to the ninth hole it was close to two-thirty. All I wanted to do was eat something and go to sleep. Much to the surprise of the others in the loop, that's exactly what I did.

There were basically two kinds of members: generous ones who bought their caddies hot dogs at the halfway house and cheap ones who bought them sodas, and did that only because they had to—it was a rule. My second loop that day was as cheap as they came, complete with a ball hound who spent more time searching for lost—free—golf balls than he did playing golf. The guy was so cheap, he didn't even buy himself anything at the halfway house. He spent the time scrounging around in the muck at the edge of the lake with a ball retriever. So I bought myself two hot dogs, ate them fast, and, as we waited for the loop ahead of us to putt out, promptly fell asleep. I was on my back between my bags, looking up at the trees, when the shades were drawn. I went down fast and I went down deep. I'd never fallen asleep during a loop before. As it turned out, no one else had either. I even had a dream: me and a blonde—Mary Butterworth? Elizabeth Brooks?—swimming in the ninth-hole lake at night, naked. My golfers got to the green before they noticed I wasn't with them. They looked around, but they couldn't see me because I was on the far side of the halfway house. There was no way Pete the Meat was going to say anything; this was history in the making, so he let them stand there and consider the situation for a while. When the loop behind us arrived at the halfway house they caught on right away and, like Pete, opted to enjoy the moment. They sat there with me asleep in the grass beside them and watched my golfers scratch their heads.

"What's the holdup?" the wits yelled down to the green.

"We've lost our caddy," the idiots yelled back. "Have you seen him?"

I awoke in confusion from my little nap and wandered through the back nine like a zombie. I didn't realize it then, but my snooze was to make me famous for a week or so. Sean told me later that even the members talked about it, and Lefty changed my name: "Let's go, Sleepy," he said, the next time he called me from the caddy yard.

I finally made it home at five-thirty. My mother was in the kitchen, preparing dinner. "Your father wants to see you," she said. "He's in the basement." She didn't say anything else; she didn't have to. A scene with the old man was inevitable after staying out all night, but I had somehow managed to block it from my mind. Normally I'd have spent the whole day dwelling on it. Instead I had enjoyed myself, a budding existentialist, oblivious to my fate.

The basement was unfinished. It had a cement floor, stone walls, and a raw, open ceiling crisscrossed with wires and pipes. My father had converted the furnace room into a workshop; the rest of the space was one big laundry room where my mother labored day and night at the Sisyphean task of keeping us all in clean clothes. A washer and dryer sat in one corner flanked by huge boxes of laundry soap and bottles of bleach. Piles of laundry spread out from around the machines in all directions, a rolling sea of shirts, pants, skirts, blouses, sheets, towels, and underwear. It was three feet deep in some spots, and several times, having become drowsy while on laundry duty, I had curled up down there and gone to sleep. Our clothes flowed endlessly through the house, like a circular river, from the basement up to the top floor and back down to the basement again. The machines ran all the time. My mother liked to stay up late reading murder mysteries and watching television by herself—precious solitude—and thought nothing of doing a few loads of wash at two in the morning.

My father was standing at his workbench, fixing a lamp. His concentration was total, even on such a little job, and he didn't look at me right away. Everything he did, he did with intensity. "If you're going to do something," he'd say, "do it right or don't bother doing it at all." In his book, doing it right meant making it perfect and twice as strong as it had to be. We had an iron-and-oak picnic table in the backyard that could withstand a nuclear attack.

"Hey, Dad, what's up?" He turned in my direction and studied me a moment without changing his expression, then went back to his lamp. The interesting thing about the old man was, instead of just getting angry at us when we fucked up, he got very, very serious, almost grave. It always made me feel strange, as though I had disappointed him in some way I couldn't understand, like I had blown it not only in the present but in the future too. I think it was because he saw us in a larger context than we saw ourselves; he saw the world waiting for us, and he knew what the world did to fuck-ups.

"Where did you sleep last night?" he asked, without looking at me.

"Over at Matt's." Now he looked, and pointed with a screwdriver he was holding.

"You live here, you don't live on Ogden Street. If your brother wants to be a bum, that's his choice. But you don't have a choice, not yet. Understand?"

"Yes."

"Remember it."

"I will."

"You better." A long minute of uncomfortable silence passed. I knew I wasn't supposed to leave yet; he was holding me there, he had something else on his mind.

"How's he doing?" he finally said.

"Who?"

"Your brother Matt."

"Oh, he's great. We looped together this morning. He made three today. Can you believe it?"

"How's that place he's living in?"

"Not bad, you know, it's small."

"Where does he eat? Besides here."

"At the diner."

"Is he drinking?"

"No, you know, just a beer now and then."

"I don't want him drinking with those Florida caddies. They drink too much. What's that one guy's name, the one whose car went in the lake?"

"Texas Billy."

"That's right. The cops tell me he's in the Oasis every night."

"I don't know."

"I don't want Matt in there. It's a rummy joint."

"He doesn't go there, Dad. He's too young anyway. He's only twenty."

"Just tell him to stay away from the place."

"I'll tell him." And then his mood softened.

"Listen, Jim."

"Yeah, Dad."

"I want you to keep an eye on him."

"Sure, Dad."

"If he needs anything, you tell me."

"Sure, Dad. He's fine, though."

"Never mind, just do what I say. Now go help your mother." I left him there in the basement, with his worries about Matt and his now-indestructible lamp.

"The main thing is, he wants you to stay out of the Oasis. It's a rummy joint." I was filling Matt in as we putted on the practice green the next morning. Every Monday was caddy day. The course was closed to the members for maintenance and the caddies were allowed to play in the morning. I had cut school with Matt's help; he called me in sick, posing as the old man, and did the same for Ned. We were a threesome.

"I've never been in the place," Matt said. "Did you tell him that?"

"Of course I did. You know, Matt, you should go see him. I think he'll talk to you now." Matt ignored me and headed for the first tee.

Ned and I were awful golfers, and our clubs didn't help us much. We were sharing a bag of antiques Ned had found in his grandfather's basement. The shafts were made of wood; the clubheads were rusty and pitted. The bag was a rotten brown canvas thing with a triangular tear in it that flapped in the breeze. It was so old it smelled old. Our footwear was a handicap also; we played in sneakers, and no matter how hard we clenched our toes we could never really get a grip on the turf. Matt was a real golfer. He wore golf shoes and had a real set of clubs he'd bought secondhand a few years before from the club pro. He had a natural swing, but after a couple of seasons of intense golf during which he won the caddy tournament, he lost interest and never got serious again.

The difficult thing about playing on caddy day was the lack of cooperation we got from the groundkeepers. If they were out in front of us on a hole, cutting the grass with the giant mower, the one they towed behind the tractor, we had to time our shots to avoid them or they would roll right over the balls and cut them to pieces. Another hazard unique to caddy day was the sprinkling system. The sprinklers ran down the center of the fairways. They were powerful things, firing water in great fifty-foot arcs. They spun in huge circles and overlapped all the way from the tees to the green. They were not supposed to be turned on until we were finished playing, but they were turned on whenever Joe Lacey felt like turning them on. To play a hole while the sprinklers were on, you hit the ball, walked down the side of the fairway, waited until the arc of water passed your ball, dashed out with club in hand, set, swung, and dashed back before the water got around to you again.

I liked golf a lot, even though I was so bad at it. All I needed was one or two good shots a round and I'd forget about all the lousy shots in between. The irony was, I was exactly the kind of shitty golfer I despised as a caddy. I even cheated the same brazen way that bad golfers cheat, by leaving a couple of strokes off my total on each hole. "Give me a six," I said, over and over again. "Same here," said Ned. "Who are you kidding?" Matt would say. "You're both getting the snowman," which was an eight.

We had the course almost completely to ourselves that day, and no sprinklers to contend with. While Ned and I trudged along like infantry, beating our balls without mercy through the rough, Matt soared. He got into a groove and made six pars in a row, from the fifth hole through the tenth, and as I watched him I saw once again how clean and simple the game could be; he hit the ball from spot to spot just so, and closed the great distances from tee to green like a surgeon closing a wound. His swing was the same each time, the key to good golf. My swing changed on every shot, the key to chaos and frustration. But it was too nice a day to flip out over something as inconsequential as my crappy golf game. I liked to walk the course even when I wasn't getting paid to do it. I liked the way it was carved out of the woods, the way the greens and the fairways and the rough and the trees all flowed together. I liked watching the ducks take off and land on the lake. It was a nice place, a peaceful place. Besides, Ned paid me a high compliment on the third green. "Hey," he said as I prepared to putt, "you drop your cigarette just like Arnold Palmer."

One of the appeals of golf is that you can do all the things you would normally do in a bar while engaging in an actual sport—you can eat, drink, talk, and smoke cigarettes. I'd been watching Palmer on television for years. He was a smoker and when he was on the green, lining up a putt, he puffed away. Then, as he stepped to the ball, he dropped his cigarette. But he didn't just drop it, he dropped it with style, with that Palmer style he brought to everything he did on a golf course. After one last drag he took the cigarette between his thumb and his fingers and held it out to his side, as if he were going to set it down in an ashtray on a table, only there was no ashtray and no table. Without taking his eyes off the line of his putt, he let the cigarette fall to the grass. Then he stepped to his ball. It was a smooth move, a truly cool move, and I had learned it without even knowing it. It was the one part of his game within my reach.

So the caddies played golf and when we got to the sixteenth green there was Mary Butterworth working in her garden. She saw us and came over to say hello. She was wearing yellow shorts and a white sleeveless blouse. Her hair was back in a ponytail and her temples were damp with perspiration; there was a sheen of sweat on her arms. "Hello, guys," she said. She stuck out her hand to shake with Matt. "Hi, Matt. I haven't seen you. How have you been?"

What I remember is how small her hand looked in his as they shook and how young she looked and how old he looked and how he smiled and how hot it seemed for a morning in early June and how there was a big tree just off the green, a big oak hanging over the green, and how we were in the shade of that tree at that moment. The tree is probably still there, but we're gone, that moment is gone, and try as I may, I can't find the tragedy in it, I can't find the loss, though I know they are there, somewhere, in that moment. They chatted— "I'm sort of between schools," I heard Matt say—while Ned and I putted out. I probably dropped my cigarette just like Arnold Palmer, but I can't remember. Matt caddied for her the next day.

8

In the fall of 1967 my father traded in the family station wagon for a Cadillac. He didn't tell us he was going to do it, he just did it. He drove off one Saturday morning in our tired Chevy and returned in a gleaming black Sedan DeVille. It was the most impulsive, impractical thing he'd ever done and he never explained it. "It's a good car," was all he said. My guess is he just got sick of buying station wagons. My mother was irked at first but quickly grew to love the Caddy. Big as it was, it was easy to drive, and the trunk held as many bags of groceries as any station wagon. It didn't matter that we couldn't all fit in it at once because we never went anywhere together anymore; Noreen and Matt were out of the house, and I dodged most of the family stuff. The interior was gray, the color of an undertaker's gloves. It had power windows and seats, an AM-FM radio, an adjustable steering wheel, and cigarette lighters everywhere. I learned how to drive in that car; it was like parallel-parking an oil tanker. There was a huge V-8 under the hood and I quickly mastered the incongruous art of laying rubber in a Cadillac. With my foot on the brake I shifted into low, revved the engine all the way up, then released the brake. The result, twenty-foot strips of stinking rubber in the street, impressed Ned no end but did not fill the backseat with fast girls, the way it was supposed to.

The old man looked great in his big black Cadillac —successful, powerful, important. Eight months after he bought it, he found out just how strong an image he projected in his new car; he was able to drive it unchallenged right into the broken heart of the matter, into Arlington National Cemetery, and watch Bobby Kennedy go into the ground.

My parents rose at six on weekday mornings and spent the hour before my father left for work down in the kitchen, talking and listening to the radio. I used to hear them as I drifted in and out of sleep. Sometimes they would have loud arguments, usually about money, but most often their voices were a comforting murmur that blended with the jingles and news reports of the local radio station. It was a sound, not words, just a sound, and we learned to read the tone of it, to detect the mood, whether serious, joking, or just routine. Not surprisingly, the mood of my parents' morning often set the mood of the day. If they fought, and woke us with their yelling, the day would go to hell, bad moods for everyone, look out below. If they laughed, and my mother was smiling when we finally made it to the kitchen, we'd share that simple morning happiness and become, for a while at least, the genuine article—a happy family.

On a Wednesday morning in early June, I woke early and knew immediately that something was wrong. There was no talking at all, and no radio. There was just the sound of the TV, very unusual. Half asleep, I made my way downstairs and found my parents side by side in front of the television.

"What happened?"

"They shot Bobby Kennedy."

"Is he dead?"

"He's dying."

My father shook hands with JFK in 1960. A picture was taken. He was proud of it, but he put it in a cardboard box in the basement because that was the way he did things. Also in a box in the basement were the medals he was awarded during World War II. He told us lots of stories about the war, but he never told us why he was given the medals. He was in the Battle of the Bulge, but the story he told us the most was about the time he and his buddies shot a cow somewhere in France and ate it. It was a good story; after they shot it, the cow rolled down a hill and it was too heavy to drag back up, so they butchered it and ate it where it landed. The Kennedy dream was of a world run at last by the brave young men who had saved it in World War II, when they were just brave young boys. The picture in the box was of two of those young men, two Democrats, both Catholic, in suits and ties, smiling, turned to the camera for a quick shot, everybody in a hurry, everybody busy, events unfolding, time flying, history waiting to be made. Kennedy beat Nixon in November and my father was reelected to the board of aldermen at the same time. How powerful they must have felt, on that other Wednesday morning, when the count was finally done and the winner—by a hair —stepped into the cold Cape Cod morning with the new decade, his own decade, stretching out before him.

We started spending two weeks each summer on the Cape; I imagine my father was not the only East Coast Democrat drawn there, consciously or not, by the Kennedy presence. We stayed in South Chatham, down on the elbow, in a small red cottage that sat like a toy in a grove of pines. Our beach was rocky and cut by swift tidal channels that fed wide marshes of waving grass. It was so different from the Jersey shore; it was another world. The strange New England weather—exquisite sunny days followed by cold rains that fell from the lowest, grayest skies I'd ever seen; misty fogs that I could feel on my skin as I walked through them—changed my idea of summer forever. We fished from the beach after dinner and built fires in the sand. We ate fried clams and drank Moxie, the ubiquitous New England soda pop that tasted to me like it had topsoil in it. There was even a small sailboat for tacking around in the mild chop of the bay. The Kennedy connection was rarely mentioned, but it was there. Hyannis Port was just a few miles down the road. In those first few summers on the Cape, the strength and the easy power of the young president were palpable. It was in the air— everybody was young, everybody was strong. It was like a dream, and like a dream, it didn't last.

I sat with my parents and watched the news. Unlike his brother, who was assassinated in black and white, Bobby Kennedy was shot down in living color. In contrast to the bleak and somber images of November 1963, the reports from Los Angeles looked garish and deranged; tall, curving palm trees waved in the background; people drove by in red convertibles. It was strange how the bullets were flying. First Martin Luther King, then Bobby Kennedy just two months later. It seemed at the time they were going to keep right on shooting people; all you could do was wonder who would be next.

We waited for him to die, and he did, the next day. That was the end of the thing, the real end of it, and the old man decided to go to Washington for the funeral. He and my mother drove down in the Cadillac. They kept driving and driving and the police kept waving them on in their long black car, through the crowds and past the barricades, right into the cemetery. They parked with all the other long black cars and took their places by the side of the grave with the senators and the congressmen and the statesmen and the diplomats. My parents stood there, genuine Kennedy Democrats who had believed in the thing and paid the price for believing, and they buried it once and for all; they put it in a hole, threw dirt on it, said a prayer over it and that was the end of it, goodbye.

The only good part was that Matt watched us while my parents were away. My father went and spoke with him and brought him back to the house. "No big deal," Matt said. But it was; the old man asked him to do something and he did it. It was a crack in the wall and the rest of us were glad to see it.

We were eating pizza from paper plates and there wasn't a glass of milk in sight, just big bottles of root beer and orange soda on the table. Jack and the twins were buzzing; Matt had promised to let them stay up as late as they wanted and they were determined to make it to midnight. As the meal ended, we heard bells ringing in the street. The twins jerked in a Pavlovian reflex. "Ice-cream man! Ice-cream man!" they shouted. They bolted from the table and out of the house. The more experienced Jack stayed behind to get the money from Matt. Out on the street, the white truck with the big ice-cream bar painted on its side was stopped beneath a streetlight. The man in the white suit was surrounded by kids. Matt and I wandered over. To our surprise, the ice-cream man was Adam Brown, onetime looper and serious card player. He hadn't been around that season and the word was his mother found out about the gambling and ordered him to quit caddying. He was happy to see us, but not too happy with his new job.

"It's pretty easy, really," he said as he handed out the goods. "I just drive around. But the pay's not so great, and there ain't no hanging out like in the caddy yard. And there sure ain't no card games. Shit, we're not even supposed to smoke when we're working." He reached deep into the truck, searching for an elusive Fudgsicle. "And poking around in this freezer all day is bad news. My hands are always cold. And to tell you the truth, the kids are a pain in the ass. Everybody wants to pay me tomorrow." He bit off the top of a Clarabelle, a chocolate-coated, bomb-shaped chunk of tutti-frutti ice cream impaled on an extra-thick Popsicle stick. "I'm eating a lot of this shit too, so I'm getting fat. And if I do meet a girl who's more than fourteen, forget about it. In this uniform, I'm a joke." A kid handed him a buck. He stuck it in his shirt pocket and punched out some nickels and dimes from the coin changer on his belt. "But the worst thing is the fucking bells. They're driving me nuts. I hear them in my sleep." When we tried to pay him, he refused to take our money. "On the house," he said. "I mean on the truck. What's new at the course?"

"Same old, same old," I said. "Little Petey's still doing it."

"That prick," said Adam. "I'd love to clean him out."

"Tell me about it."

"Maybe I'll stop down."

A kid came riding up on his bike. "Hey ice-cream man," he said, "how come you didn't do Cutler Street yet? We been waiting for you."

"This ain't my regular route, kid," Adam said. "I'll get there. Gimme a chance."

"Well, my mom said to hurry up or she's gonna call the company."

The kid circled us once and rode off. Adam shook his head. "Good Humor my ass," he said as he climbed into the truck. "Catch you later."

After the ice-cream man left, Matt organized a big game of hide-and-go-seek with all the kids on the street. The twins were leery of the dark, so I hid with them. We tucked ourselves in behind the shrubs right in front of our own house, where they felt safe.

Matt was It. He leaned against the telephone pole that was Home, covered his eyes and counted to one hundred. Then he set off in search of everyone. Of course, he knew every good hiding place for blocks around. We'd been playing the game for years. We knew every inch of every backyard. We had climbed every tree, been in every garage, under every back porch and over every fence. We had shoveled the snow off all the sidewalks, cut all the grass, raked all the leaves. We'd been in all the houses—as friends, as paperboys, and as magazine-subscription salesmen raising money for the missionaries. It was our neighborhood; we owned it.

We sat there in the shadows and watched Matt wander up and down the street. Every now and then he'd roust someone and they'd scream and make a dash for the telephone pole. Eventually he found them all. "We're the last ones," I whispered to the twins. They shivered with excitement. Matt had seen us from the start but had left us to win the game. He started walking slowly in our direction. "Now where could Jill and Maura be?" he said aloud. He came across the front lawn, heading right for us. "They've got to be around here somewhere." It was too much for the twins, they screeched and leapt from the bushes. Matt chased them in circles toward Home, and when they made it safely he swooped in and lifted them off the ground. He spun them around and around, one under each arm. The other kids started jumping up and down. "Spin me, Matt, spin me!" they yelled. But he held on to his little sisters and they held on to him and they danced off together down the street, to the next streetlight and the next and the next, spinning slower and slower as they went. By the time they reached the end of the block their movements were as gentle as a waltz.

In spite of their plans to stay up all night, the kids were asleep by ten-thirty. Matt and I sat in the quiet house and watched the late news together. First we saw the funeral. We didn't know our parents had gotten so close to the center of the thing, or we might have spotted them. It was the big graveyard we saw, dead soldiers, rolling acres of headstones, thousands of small American flags stirring in the breeze; the widow, the children, the whole depressing machinery of royal American death, Kennedy death. Then came a report from the war. We saw some American soldiers standing in a clump of trees and tall grass. It looked like there was something going on somewhere nearby and they were trying to figure out exactly where and what it was. They were tense and alert, turning in different directions and listening hard. The chirp of gunfire sounded in the background. They kept looking around, talking to each other, pointing. A guy with a radio on his back crouched in the grass while another guy talked into it. The camera work was shaky. At one point, they all ducked. It wasn't real clear what the story was. It was just these few worried-looking American soldiers trying to figure something out. It was familiar stuff, the kind of thing we'd been watching for years, except now, with Matt maybe going there, it looked different. It wasn't just something on TV. I looked at their faces. All of a sudden one of them stood up, pointed his rifle through the grass, and started firing. Then another guy did the same thing.

Then they all did it. It didn't look to me like they were aiming very carefully—one guy stayed low in the grass and just held his rifle over his head while he fired—but they kept blasting away at something. Then they were gone and a commercial came on.

"What do you think?" I said. We hadn't talked about the draft or anything since his first day back in town.

"About what?" Matt answered. I felt a vague anger.

"Come on, Matt. You know what I'm talking about. The war." He took a sip of beer—we were living it up—before he answered.

"It's weird, isn't it," he said, "watching it on television? I mean, it's so unreal, it makes you wonder what the real thing is like. I mean, the pictures are real, you're seeing things that are actually happening, but it's not real. But you know, because of the pictures, that there's something real going on there, right? So you wonder what that is. You know what I mean?"

"Yeah, I guess."

He pointed at the television. "There's something happening, but that's not it. You can't see it on TV. There's no way to know what it is except to go there and find out for yourself."

"Is that what you want to do?"

"I don't know."

"Well, I know what's happening. A war is happening, that's what. Guys are getting killed."

Matt looked at me a moment, then he nodded his head in agreement. "That's right," he said. "You're right."

"And I think it's a waste."

It was too late; Matt had connected with the war. In just a few weeks he had gone from feigned indifference—his trademark attitude—to intellectual curiosity. Naturally, when he finally took an interest the contrary bastard got it wrong. The rest of the country was sick of the goddamn thing, but not Matt. He was drawn to it. Eventually, I realized, he'd find his place in it. He'd decide what part the war was supposed to play in his life and that would be that. When he stepped into the jungle, he'd have a plan, and it wouldn't be anything as simple as merely staying alive.

"How can you be in the Army, anyway?" I asked. "You can't even stand being in college." I was ready to talk about it, but he changed the subject on me.

"I'm going to give Mary Butterworth lessons," he said. "Did I tell you that?"

"What?"

"We worked it out the other day. Every Tuesday morning. I carry her bag, help her with her game, she pays me extra."

"You dog."

"Oh yeah. It's hard work, but what the fuck. That's what life's all about, right? Think quick!" He tossed his empty beer can at me; I caught it with one hand. He pulled himself off the couch and headed for the kitchen. "See who's on Carson. You want another beer?"

School ended and summer came on. I was at the golf course every day. There were better jobs and there were worse jobs. I wasn't a good enough swimmer to be a lifeguard, so I couldn't sit around all day surrounded by girls in bathing suits and work on my tan. And I wasn't old enough for construction work, so I couldn't make big money and develop big muscles while drinking beer. On the other hand, I knew guys who spent their summers working in supermarkets for minimum wage, stocking the shelves and hosing down the vegetables. A lot of them had bad skin and all of them had to wear greasy-looking uniforms and plastic name tags, much too high a price to pay for the privilege of hanging around the checkout girls. Probably the best summer job I ever heard of was beach photographer. A friend of Matt's actually was paid to walk up and down the beach taking pictures of people. The pictures were mounted in souvenir plastic viewers that cost a buck. I met the guy on a day trip to the beach with Matt; half the reason we went was to confirm the existence of the job. Of course, the guy carried himself like an heir to the throne. He was so content he could barely talk. "Well," he said wearily, dragging himself up off the sand, "I gotta go to work." We watched in amazement as he wandered off, camera in hand, wearing nothing but a bathing suit and a pair of sunglasses. He was fired after three weeks for being lazy.

It wasn't beach photography, but there was a lot to be said for caddying as a summer job. The money was good and there was no clock to punch and no uniform to wear. I had plenty of friends around and I could smoke and play cards. I was outdoors all the time, so I got a good tan on my face and arms, which was all I really needed. And I got to know plenty of old guys who could buy me beer. On top of all that, I developed endurance from all the walking; I was healthy in spite of myself.

When you start a loop, you can't believe you'll ever finish; it's such a long way to go. Eighteen holes, four hours, six wandering miles at a slow pace. Walking uphill, walking downhill, into the woods and out onto the fairways, which are wide and hot under the August sun, cold and windblown in the late fall. It was an elemental job, carrying heavy objects long distances. Two loops was twelve miles of walking, talking, thinking, smoking, watching the ball, watching your feet. When you caddied, your head was naturally bowed, as though you were entering a church over and over again, so you were always looking down at your feet, your faithful feet, sliding forward across the grass in order, left right, left right, marking off the miles one step at a time. I walked to the golf course, I walked around the golf course, and I walked home again. I walked around town, I walked to the store, I walked to the movies on Friday nights. It was basic transportation, one foot in front of the other, the shoe-leather express. "What kind of car you got?" went the old joke. "I got a Chevrolet," was the answer, the word pronounced loosely, without the R. "I chev out the left one and lay down the right one." Walking in the morning and the afternoon and the evening. Just walking along in my physical body, moving through the air, through space, contemplating the slow unrolling of the familiar scenery, the world passing under my feet in small pieces; I leave it behind me. Load those golf bags on my shoulders. Some caddies, you wouldn't bet they could make it to the first green. But they fooled you. The Shuffler was slow, very slow, he just shuffled along, but he'd shuffle around the world and keep on going when he passed you, too. Some caddies were skinny from eating bad and drinking too much, scrawny drinkers, jumpy like rabbits. In the morning they'd be out there moaning for the first few holes, suffering with hangovers, ready to die. Then it would start to lift and you'd see them go through the cycle, coming out of it, starting to feel better, starting to get happy, thinking about getting some money and then something to drink again. You'd see them pass through that shadow and come into the sunlight, that drinker's sunshine, when he knows he feels better and he knows he will drink again. He will walk his loop, then walk to the bar, walk to the liquor store, and get his drink.

On Tuesdays, when the women played, the caddies matched up with the members' wives. It was an interesting combination. There they'd be, in their pastel outfits, with their hair all done up, skittering around like a pack of poodles, and there we'd be, hound dogs to a man. Texas Billy had an elaborate set of manners he rolled out for the occasion, complete with deep bows and a sickly-sweet smile that never left his face. "A very nice shot indeed," he would say as yet another bad drive skidded along the ground. Or, "I'm sorry to say it, ma'am, but that ball appears to be just a wee bit out of bounds. Perhaps you should hit another." I think it was a nervous reaction; he'd been married a few times and was wary of women in general. Man o' War took the opposite approach and never opened his mouth, except to talk to himself. He just walked down the center of the fairway, mumbling, while his perfumed charges quietly complained to each other about him. I didn't go for the women too much myself, actually. There was only one Mary Butterworth, and only a handful were close to her age. The rest were closer to my mother's age and they seemed ridiculous to me, because I knew my mother would never waste her time on a golf course. More exactly, my mother didn't have the time to play golf, or the money, and women who did, I decided, could not be taken seriously.

One Tuesday, as Texas Billy and I got to the first green with our group of bad golfers, I saw Matt and Mary over on the third fairway, about a hundred and fifty yards away. She had an uphill lie for her third shot and Matt was demonstrating the proper stance. He was saying something and she was laughing and even at that distance it was easy to see they were comfortable together. There was more to it than her usual friendly manner with people. It was the way they shared space, the way she leaned toward him slightly as she laughed; the small, critical distance that keeps most human beings apart was closing between them. They were enjoying each other.

It was an overcast day, and when we got to the fourth tee the skies darkened suddenly and opened up. It was a heavy summer downpour; we dashed to a shelter and were soon joined by another group that included One Eye and Red Ryder. The twelve of us— eight lady golfers and four caddies—huddled together and waited for the rain to stop. But it didn't stop. It got worse by the minute. As the ladies gossiped, Billy and One Eye started talking about storms they had seen. Pretty soon they were arguing about which was worse—a hurricane or a tornado.

"I'd rather be in a hurricane anytime," Billy said. "A hurricane is a vacation from a tornado." We had gravitated to the outer edge of the shelter, just in under the roof. The golfers were behind us; we were protecting them from the blowing rain.

"You can get away from a tornado," One Eye said. "You can see it coming for miles."

"A tornado will always kill more people than a hurricane," Billy said. "But sometimes it won't. They're funny things. One time in Oklahoma City, a tornado picked me right up off a bed, took the mattress out from under me, and dropped me back on the springs, just like that."

"I seen a palm tree go down the middle of the street like a rocket," said One Eye. "Six feet off the ground, right down the middle of the street and around the corner, just like that, like somebody was steering the goddamn thing."

"I seen a dog fly," Red Ryder said.

I looked out into the rain and saw Matt and Mary all the way over on the other side of the fifth fairway, at the edge of the woods. They were under a tree, sharing an umbrella. I didn't see the rest of their group. I yelled out to them. Matt saw me and waved, then waved for me to join them. I sprinted into the rain, across the slippery grass, splashing all the way.

"Look at you, Jim," said Mary, as I skidded in under their tree, "you're drenched." Matt handed me a towel. "That's an interesting crowd you ran out on," he said. "What are we missing?"

"The usual," I said. "Red's flying dog."

"What's that?" Mary asked.

"A windstorm in northern Africa," Matt explained. "Red saw a dog get carried away. It's his favorite weather story."

"Is it true?"

"I'm sure it is," Matt said, "or something like it. You should ask him about it some time."

"So," Mary said, "here I am, stranded with the Mooney brothers." She studied our faces. "You have the same eyes. Are they from your mother's side or your father's?"

"My mother's," I said.

"How nice."

Actually, I was never very good at seeing those kinds of details, but we'd been over it all so many times over the years I knew the list. Except for Jack, who looked exactly like my father, and Erin, who looked exactly like my mother, we were a mixed bag. My mother's eyes, my father's nose, my mother's chin, my father's ears, and so on. With eight kids in the family, including identical twins, we were like a research project in genetics.

"My mother had the most extraordinary cheekbones," said Mary, "but unfortunately I didn't get them. I can't imagine what my life would have been like if I had. I'd probably be living in Paris." It was supposed to sound silly, but I knew her mother had died the year before. She paused, and then went on. "It's strange, isn't it, the way people get together and make new people who look like them, but not quite? It's so . . ." She searched for the word.

"Natural," said Matt. She looked at him.

"Yes," she said, "that's it. Natural. Strange and natural."

"Like this rain," he said.

"Just like this rain," she echoed. I didn't know what they were talking about and I don't think they did either. It sounded as though they were saying whatever came into their heads. They drifted into her golf game next.

"My tee shot on the second . . ." she said.

"That was your left arm, like I told you," Matt answered.

"It felt so different."

"That's because you did it right."

"So that's what it was. I did it right." Then, because we were all standing so close, she noticed how tall I was.

"Why, Jim," she said, "look how tall you are." She made us stand back-to-back. "He's got you by half an inch, Matt."

It went on like that, and then we didn't speak for a while. The incredible rain drummed down on the umbrella and fell noisily in the woods behind us. I looked out across the empty course; the sky and the earth were one, joined by the rain, and everything glowed as if lit from within. As the rain fell even harder the world shrank around us, our small green world, luminescent, lost. That powerful rain, pouring down on us from such a low heaven, astonished me; for the first and only time in my life I could conceive the great Flood. Across the fairway, Billy and the others were a blur. "Billy," I said aloud. It was going to be a sentence, but the word sounded so strange, muffled by the rain, that I didn't say anything else. Then Mary spoke. "It's never going to stop," she said with drama in her voice. "What will become of us?" We laughed and I looked down at the ground. My feet were underwater. "We'll all be washed away," I said, and no one disagreed.

But we were not. The moment passed, the downpour eased, and we sloshed back across the course to the clubhouse. Mary offered to drive us home. I passed—there was a card game starting—but Matt, Billy, Red Ryder, and One Eye all crowded into her white car. I watched them drive off, wipers going, windows fogged by rain. Maybe she'll invite them all to dinner, I thought, and surprise Sean.

There was a small soda fountain in the hospital on Jefferson Avenue where I used to stop now and then on my way home from the course. It had a horseshoe-shaped counter. The girl who worked there wasn't very good-looking or very friendly, but she had a big chest and if you were sitting on the right stool you could get a pretty good look down her blouse when she bent over to scoop the ice cream. Ned liked her and tried to talk to her but he could never find a subject she was interested in. He'd go on and on about an album, a movie, a trip to the beach, anything and everything, but she'd never react. She'd just stand there chewing her gum. When he had finished his rap and the inevitable uncomfortable silence had descended upon us, she'd lurch into motion. "Youse want anything else?" she'd say, pulling the check pad from her apron.

It was a different story when I was alone. She'd

serve me and return to her magazine while I enjoyed my ice-cream soda in peace. Sometimes I'd have a book with me—I'd been working my way through the James Bond series since 1965—other times I'd just sit there and think. That's what I was doing, thinking, when Elizabeth Brooks walked in and sat down across from me. It was the day of the downpour and we were the only customers in the place, so we had to look at each other. She seemed to recognize me, but I could see that she wasn't sure why. I gave her a little nod and half a smile. Then she remembered.

"Hey, it's you," she said, "the guy from my party." She came around the counter and hopped onto the stool next to me. She was wearing a pink candy-striper uniform. I'd never called her, of course, though I did look up her number. To my amazement, she was excited to see me.

"This is great. I'm so glad to see you. What's your name? You know, the doctors said you saved Todd's life. Isn't that amazing? But nobody knew who you were. What are you doing here?"

Because of the party, her parents had grounded her for the entire summer and ordered her to do volunteer work at the hospital. She couldn't drive and she was forbidden to see certain friends, including her old boyfriend, which was okay with her, she said, because he wasn't her boyfriend anymore anyway. She went on like that, filling me in on the details of what she called her horrible life as if I were an old friend. It was nice, but I didn't know what to say. As the stories piled up, I realized we were total strangers; I didn't know any of her friends and she didn't know any of mine. I also realized that my dream girl couldn't stop talking.

Maybe she was bored with her hospital work, or starved for companionship. Whatever it was, she just talked and talked. I hadn't expected that. I had assumed she was the quiet type. When I pictured us together, it was always in silence. Of course, she was the center of a large social set, one of the most popular girls around, so it was understandable that she talked a lot. And it certainly took the pressure off me; all I had to do was look interested. Her beautiful jaw flapped nonstop for twenty minutes. I drifted off to a very nice place where I could see her perfect body and smell her faint perfume but I couldn't hear a word she said. I returned to earth when she reached out and touched my nose.

"Where did you get the cute sunburn?" she asked. It was my turn to talk.

"It's from caddying," I said. "I'm a caddy."

"I think my dad did that when he was growing up," she said. "Is it fun?"

"It's all right. You know, it's a job."

"Where do you work?"

"Colonial Valley. Across the road."

Naturally, she knew a lot of the members' kids and had been swimming at the club a few times. The fact that I was a looper and not a member didn't seem to bother her. She plunged right into a long story about a golf lesson she had taken when she was twelve or something. She had the tiniest hint of a southern accent, and when I got a chance I asked her about it. Turned out she'd been born in New Orleans while her father was in law school and had lived there until she was eight. She was launching into the family history—Mom and Dad were originally from Chicago—when another candy-striper showed up looking for her. She quickly scrawled her phone number on a napkin and stuck it in my shirt pocket.

"Will you call me, Jim? Tonight?"

"Sure."

"Promise?"

"I promise."

She jumped off her stool and kissed me on the cheek. My highly trained and sensitive shoulder registered fleeting contact with her breasts.

"You're sweet," she said. Her hand lingered on my back. "And you're soaking wet. You get home, now, before you catch cold." I watched her walk away; her candy-striped butt was a lot cuter than my nose. So what if she was a little noisy? Maybe if I opened my mouth once in a while, she wouldn't have to talk so much. I resolved to think of something to say to her.

9

By some mechanism I never fully understood, Elizabeth and I became a couple over the next few weeks. At the same time, though Matt's situation didn't change, the tension eased. He and my father let their truce stand and he started having dinner with the family at least once a week. At the golf course, I convinced Sean that he could win the club championship if he wanted to and to my surprise he decided to go after it. And though my luck at cards didn't improve, Lefty finally recognized me as one of his key men and I started getting more and better loops than ever before. Things were pretty good, it was a pretty good time, a good time in the summer, summertime, high summer, with long summer days and even longer summer nights. The warm air of summer and the deep greens of summer and the cool waters of summer enveloped me. Spring is more promising, fall is more powerful, and winter is more dramatic, but summer is the season of freedom and the danger that goes with it. In the summer, people do what they want to do because they want to do it, because it's easy and there's time to do it and all you need, maybe, is a light jacket to get you through the night.

With Elizabeth, it started with phone calls, long phone calls during which she would talk for an hour or so about her day and then ask me how I was. I was fine, of course, and amazed to be the object of her attention. After a couple of meetings more at the hospital soda fountain, she invited me to her house. Her father was easing up on her a little and I made it on to the short list of people she was allowed to have over. And so it was that I found myself on a fine summer afternoon pursuing the new and exciting vocation of cheerleading coach and critic. In fact, I was being inspected by two of Elizabeth's friends; they were checking me out to see if I was suitable summer-boyfriend material. That meant I was subject to rejection, but at least they had a nice way of going about it. If you are going to be inspected, you might as well be inspected by earnest and attractive young cheerleaders who are willing to jump up and down, turn cartwheels, and do splits on the lawn in front of you while they decide your fate. And if there's a hammock in the shade and a pitcher of iced tea on hand as well, so much the better.

Actually, the treatment I received made me uncomfortable at first. It felt strange lying there like some kind of cheesy pooh-bah while the girls performed. It occurred to me that they might be playing a joke on me—"Let's stick him in the hammock, give him a show and see how he reacts"—but the scene was too straightforward for that. It didn't have that extra edge to it, that little touch of meanness that such jokes involve. It was an honest afternoon; Elizabeth and her friends were sincerely practicing the cheerleading arts—Blessed Virgin, the all-girl school they attended, provided the cheerleaders for St. Paul's, an all-boy school—and every now and then, when they asked me what I thought of this move or that move, I told them the truth: "It looked okay to me." But it was also a demonstration of their power over me, a simple little demonstration of their strength and my weakness. I was watching them and enjoying it, but they were watching me, too, and there was no doubt about who was in charge. The inescapable fact was that I had been summoned to that backyard because I was being considered for a position of some prominence—Elizabeth Brooks's boyfriend. Reasonable good looks and a working knowledge of first aid had gotten me to that point, but now the real issues had to be confronted: Did I fit in? Was I cool? Could I handle being in the presence of such socially important and good-looking females on a regular basis, or was I just another geek? Did I know how to watch cheerleading practice without drooling?

About half an hour into the ordeal I went to the kitchen for more iced tea, and when I came out of the house I had a copy of *Sports Illustrated* with me. The rest of the time I alternated between the magazine and the girls. I managed to locate the fine line between being too attentive to their healthy, leaping bodies and not attentive enough. The hard part was remembering to turn the page every now and then.

I knew I had passed the test when, after her friends left, Elizabeth took me up to her room. It was the ultimate girl's room, a genuine virgin's lair, with flowered wallpaper, lace curtains, a pink-skirted dressing table, and dozens of dolls and stuffed animals scattered around. In the center of the room, like a big, soft island, stood a white four-poster bed. We sat on the edge of it while she showed me a scrapbook she'd been keeping since she was a little kid. Fifteen minutes later I was slumped beside her, bored as a tollbooth clerk and all out of "hmmms," when suddenly she took my hand and the next thing I knew we were kissing.

"I really like you, Jim," she said.

"I like you too, Elizabeth," I replied. "I like you a lot."

It was the middle of the afternoon. Not only was I finally going to feel bare tit, I was going to see it as well. All I had to do was get her prone. I leaned back as casually as I could, but she held her position. Instead of kissing her I was staring at her back; I could see the outline of her bra strap, with the slight puff of material around the hooks.

"You're different than the boys I usually go out with, you're more of a gentleman."

It was not a word I wanted to hear. I wasn't interested in being different from the boys she usually went out with. They were, I was quite sure, as horny a pack of curs as ever pissed on a telephone pole and I wanted her to think of me the way she probably thought of them—as a rapacious beast. I didn't want to be a gentleman, I wanted to be an animal in need of suck.

"My mother loves the way you talk on the phone."

There was another word I didn't want to hear.

"What do you mean?"

"When you call, you always say 'Hello, this is Jim Mooney calling. Is Elizabeth there?'"

"Yeah, and what do other people say?"

"Oh, you know, 'Hi, is Lizbeth there.' 'Hi, can I talk to Lizbeth?' They don't identify themselves or anything. They just mumble. Not you, though."

It was true, my parents had cursed us with manners. Sit up straight, keep your elbows off the table, chew with your mouth closed, say excuse me, hold the door, say please, thank you, no thank you, you're welcome. "Always be a gentleman," my father told Matt and me over and over, and what he meant was be sensitive to the feelings of others. They were relentless about it and it paid off; though like most kids we seethed with natural rudeness, we were basically well-behaved. Elizabeth and I kissed for an hour or so, perched awkwardly on the edge of the bed, and then I left. I had a girlfriend at last, a famous bombshell, but there'd be no BT for me that day for the same reason there had never been BT for me—because I was a nice guy.

The Fourth of July was a big deal at Colonial Valley, a major American holiday with flags, alcohol, black powder, sunshine, and burnt meat in abundance. The idea was to eat a lot, drink a lot, and make a lot of noise. It was good for us caddies because we were generally allowed to eat and drink along with everybody else and, because drunk people are almost always looser with their money than sober people, the tips were better. The main event was a "shotgun" golf tournament, where they send groups of golfers out to every tee and start them all off at once by firing a shotgun into the air. Shotgun tournaments were chaotic affairs. Lefty hated them because he had to pull all the bags and assign all the caddies at once. The worst thing that could happen to a caddy was to be assigned to start on a hole all the way out in one of the far corners of the course. You'd have to walk out there, walk a loop, and then walk all the way back in again. The good thing was there were barbecue grills scattered around the course and roving bars loaded on golf carts. It was one day when nobody cared about their score; the members tossed firecrackers during backswings and played other juvenile tricks on one another as they drank and ate their way around the course.

Because every hole was jammed from the start, shotgun loops took at least five hours. I caddied for Sean and Randy Goodman. Bob Hill was the other caddy in the foursome. We teed off about ten or so, and it was a long, slow, hot day. Sean, drinking beer and margaritas, had a pretty good load on by noon. I had a minor beer buzz of my own.

"Mary tells me your brother's going to let himself get drafted," Sean said. We were walking side by side out ahead of the others. We were each carrying a cup of beer.

"It looks that way," I said. "He's sick of school."

"She wants me to talk to him." This was interesting. Mary had told Matt that Sean never talked about the war, that he'd never even told her how he got shot.

"Well . . ." I said. He looked at me.

"I don't do that," he said. I just nodded. "But you can give him a message."

"Okay." He took a sip from his beer before he spoke.

"Tell him he's making a big mistake." I waited for him to continue, but that was it, that was all he said.

"I told him that already. Everybody's told him that." I was disappointed, and he knew it.

"And now I'm telling him," he said. "That makes it unanimous."

"Yeah, sure."

He stopped walking. "You want more than that?"

"Well, you were there."

He studied my face for a moment; his bloodshot eyes narrowed in thought. "All right, then," he said, and his words came fast. "Tell him it's the worst fucking place in the world. Tell him he's meat. Tell him God's a mean fuck who can't wait to hear him scream." He finished his beer with a quick swig; his final words came slower. "Tell him if he goes there he'll die."

I was stunned; it was as if he punched me.

Sean turned and saw Goodman starting his backswing. "Hit the ball you fat fuck," he yelled. Goodman shanked it as Sean cackled with glee.

"Fuck you," I said. Sean turned back to face me. We stood there in that terrible noon heat.

"Fuck me," he said with a nod, as though he were agreeing with me. "Fuck me." He looked down the fairway. His breathing seemed uneven; I think we were both feeling a little dizzy. "I'm sorry, Jim," he said. "He's your brother and I'm sorry I said what I said. I had a bad time over there, that's all. I'm sorry."

We increased our drinking considerably after that and by the time we made it to our last hole we were boiled.

"I'm gonna have a stroke," Sean said as he stood in the fairway, waiting to hit. "I ought to jump in the fucking lake. It looks nice, doesn't it?" The lake, surrounded by trees, looked deep and cool in the shady distance.

"I think that's a great idea," said Goodman. "And to make it worth your while, I'll give you twenty bucks if you do it."

"You cheap fuck, Goodman," Sean said, "make it fifty."

Just then we heard the crack of a starting pistol and loud cheering; there was a little water carnival going on up at the pool.

"Okay," Goodman said, looking toward the pool, "I'll make it fifty, but forget the lake. You have to go off the high dive. With your clothes on. Right now."

Sean thought about it a moment.

"I'll do it," he said, "for a hundred."

"No way," Goodman said.

"Okay, forget it."

"You're on, asshole."

"Fuck you, let's go."

Since most of the dads were still out on the course, the crowd at the pool was composed largely of moms, kids, and grandparents. We waited outside the fence as Sean, smiling and shaking hands with everyone, made his way toward the diving boards. Nobody paid much attention to him at first, not until he started climbing the ladder to the high dive. A buzz ran through the crowd as people laughed and pointed. Goodman stood beside me, rubbing his hands together.

"Go on, you crazy bastard," he said, "climb."

As Sean reached the top of the ladder, the head lifeguard, a member's son who took his job seriously, stood at the foot of the ladder and called up to him. "Okay, Mr. Butterworth, sir, that's enough now. Would you climb back down please."

Sean ignored him and walked out to the end of the board. The lifeguard went up the ladder. Sean started to entertain the crowd, which responded with enthusiasm. He teetered back and forth, almost falling, then caught himself. He sat down and dangled his legs over the water, his golf spikes glinting in the sun. He lay back as if asleep, arms out to the sides. Then he stood up and prepared to dive, testing the spring in the board, bending at the knees, throwing his arms up over his head. The lifeguard moved out on the board toward Sean.

"Come on now, Mr. Butterworth," he said. "This is a really bad idea. Somebody could get hurt."

"Get lost, kid," Sean said. "I'm trying to win some money here."

Sean called out to the crowd.

"What'll it be, folks? Swan dive? Cannonball? Back flip?"

Then the lifeguard made his mistake. He leaned down and spoke to the other two guards on the deck below him. "I want everybody out of the pool," he said. "Now."

And so a stupid stunt became an ugly scene. All the people climbed out of the water and stood staring as Sean and the earnest lifeguard confronted each other high over the empty pool. With the sudden quiet you could hear Sean's spikes digging into the fiberglass diving board as he turned to face the kid.

"What the hell are you trying to prove, son?"

"Nothing, Mr. Butterworth. Could you come down, please?"

Sean was instantly disgusted with the whole scene.

"We're just having fun, kid. That's all. Why do you have to be such a little prick about it?"

"I'm responsible for what happens here," the lifeguard said. He was going to continue for a while, but Sean cut him off.

"Fuck off, punk. You don't know the meaning of the word."

Sean's language actually drove some people back a few steps; I saw a couple of mothers reach down and put their hands over their children's ears.

"Ladies and gentlemen," Sean yelled, "for my next trick I will toss this supercilious little shit into the pool below."

As the lifeguard took a step forward, Sean leaned out, grabbed his arm, and yanked. With a shout, the lifeguard fell off the board and down into the water. It was an awful, degenerate sight and it stunned the crowd into silence. Then Sean started bouncing up and down, higher and higher, as the board banged louder and louder. His spikes were cutting deep into the fiberglass; I could see little chunks of it tearing loose and floating down to the surface of the water. Someone in the crowd started booing and in a moment they were all doing it. Finally, when it looked as though he were about to snap the board in half, Sean launched himself up and out into the air. He hung there for just a moment, a mean, crazy drunk in flight; then gravity got him and pulled him down. I turned away just before he hit the water.

A few days later I met Matt for dinner at the diner.

"So," he said, as I slid into the booth across from him, "have you heard the latest about your buddy Sean, the Olympic diver?"

"What's that?"

"His wife left him."

Matt was clearly pleased.

"No shit."

"Yes shit. She moved back to her father's house."

"She told you?"

"I heard about it. I haven't seen her yet."

I wasn't surprised. No one was surprised. The surprise was that it hadn't happened sooner.

"So that's it," I said.

"That's it," said Matt. "She dumped him."

"I wonder if they'll still play golf?" I said. Matt laughed.

"You are such a fucking looper," he said, shaking his head. "You ready to order?"

Matt played it safe with the hot roast-beef sandwich. I took a chance with a fresh trout from the fish tank they kept near the front door. It tasted like metal.

"How's your romance going?" Matt asked.

"Pretty good. We're going on an actual date next week."

"It's about time."

"Yeah. She's been working on her old man for a month now, telling him what a good Catholic I am."

"I'll bet. Where are you going to take her?"

"I don't know. We might double with Ned. He's got Billy's Cadillac running again. I'm going to check it out tomorrow." The waitress arrived with dessert; I had decided to smother the trout with a banana split.

"You mean the one that went in the lake?"

"Yeah. He's been working on it since the spring."

"That's great. Girls love Cadillacs. Who's Ned taking?"

"The girl from the soda fountain."

"The one with the tits?"

"Yeah. Her name's Tina."

"Sounds like you guys are in for a hot one."

"Let's hope so."

"What do you think?" Ned asked proudly. But I couldn't think at all. I could only look at the thing, trying to see it and all of its extraordinary details. He had painted it flat gray, primer-gray, and where once it had looked like a rocket ship, now it looked like a battleship. It was riding low and not quite level—it listed to starboard just a bit. He had replaced the missing tail fin, but the body work was lumpy and the fit wasn't right; the fin had an odd angle to it that threw the whole car out of line, the automotive equivalent of a nervous tic. In keeping with the new color scheme, which meant no color at all, Ned had opted for blackwall tires, ten-dollar retreads, the very popular Maypop brand, which, as the famous slogan points out, "may pop any time." In contrast to the hard-edged industrial theme of the exterior, the interior was homey and damp, like Grandma's house after a flood. The major feature was a bed-spread that Ned had painstakingly installed in place of the old headliner. It was an artful arrangement of duct tape and flannel that drooped just so and lent the inside of the car a soft, tentlike atmosphere. The floor of the car was strewn with old pieces of carpet, and the backseat, which refused to dry out com-pletely, was covered with an enormous Budweiser beach towel. The radio didn't work, but Ned had taped a little transistor job to the dashboard, with duct tape, of course. There was access to the trunk through the fold-down armrest in the middle of the backseat and a hole in the floor for beer-dumping in the event of a police emergency. By far the strangest thing about the interior of the car was the colony of fruit flies that had taken up residence there. We couldn't figure out where they came from, but they were always around. I guess they huddled down and hung on when the car moved, because, tiny as they were, they never seemed to blow away. Whenever the car stopped, even if it was just for a light, they appeared out of nowhere, circling slowly in the air.

The mechanics of the car were as interesting and idiosyncratic as the aesthetics. There was no reverse gear, so every trip involved a lot of planning, and parking lots were avoided as a rule. Only six of the eight cylinders worked. The car tended to stall, so whenever he came to a stoplight Ned had to throw it into neutral and race the engine. The brakes, though better than they had been the day Wayne rolled into the lake, were not that great; there was much vigorous pumping involved, and the car had to be on level ground to stop, so hills were also out of the question. The engine burned an extraordinary amount of oil—Ned kept a case of the stuff in the trunk—and put out an iridescent purple smoke that was actually more vapor than it was smoke; everywhere he went in his big machine, Ned trailed a hot petroleum mist that glistened in the sunlight. The lights worked, but the turn signals, the windshield wipers, and speedometer were all nonfunctional. The electric windows didn't work either—they were down forever—so rainstorms were another worry.

I agreed to the double date reluctantly; he was so fucking proud of the thing, I couldn't say no.

"So you're the young man I've been hearing so much about," Elizabeth's father said. He shook my hand and flashed a quick, tight smile. The smile was for the benefit of Elizabeth and her mother, who were standing beside us in the living room; he was being the nice guy he no doubt had promised them he would be. But the cool glare in his eyes and the extra little squeeze he put into the handshake—my knuckles clicked together like marbles in his grip—were just for me. He was sending me a message, the same message that the fathers of beautiful young females have been sending to horny young males since the beginning of time. "It would be a pleasure to break your back," was the gist of it. If Jesus Christ himself had come to pick up Elizabeth he would have gotten the same treatment. Her father didn't like me because he knew what I was after and I didn't like him because he didn't like me. If we were elk we would have butted heads until one of us fell over dead. But we were humans, so we spent a few strained moments chatting and exchanging telepathic hostilities, as Elizabeth and her mother stood there smiling.

"Daddy likes you," Elizabeth said to me as we left the house, "I can tell." He likes me all right, I thought, he'd like to run me over with his car. She held my hand as we crossed the lawn. "And mother thinks you're cute." She stepped close and gave me a peck on the cheek, pressing her breasts against my arm in the process. "So do I." She stayed close and her breasts did too. I could have walked around like that all night, but there was Ned's car down at the end of the driveway. Elizabeth stopped in her tracks when she saw it. She stood there staring at it, much as I had done the first time I laid eyes on it.

"I thought we were going out in a Cadillac," she said.

"It is a Cadillac. It's a 1960 Coupe DeVille. It used to belong to Arnold Palmer."

The sound of the transistor radio reached us, weak and tinny, as if it were being broadcast from across the universe. Actually, since Ned hadn't dared to turn the engine off, the thin noise was emerging from an oily cloud of exhaust that was slowly engulfing the cul-de-sac. In the shadows of the front seat I could see Tina in profile, nodding her head to the beat.

"Is it safe?"

"Sure. Ned's a great mechanic. Come on."

The passenger-side door was a little balky; Tina had to bang it with her shoulder while I pulled on the handle to open it.

I hadn't told Elizabeth about Tina, I just said we were doubling with my best friend. She was climbing into the backseat when she recognized her. She hesitated a moment, half in and half out of the car. "Oh, hi," she said. "You work at the hospital, don't you?"

"That's me," Tina said.

"Tina, right?"

"Yeah, right."

Tina was not in a great mood. Ned had promised to take her out in a Cadillac. That was the only reason she agreed to the date, and she did not consider Texas Billy's car a Cadillac. "Who's he?" she asked when Ned mentioned the Arnold Palmer connection. "He's one of the greatest golfers who ever lived," Ned answered. "Oh yeah?" she said. "Well his car's about the biggest piece of shit I've ever seen." Tina lived with her mother in a beat-up old house that had been divided into small apartments. It had a big patch of hard dirt in front of it, where the lawn was supposed to be, and we stood there in the dust for a few dramatic moments while she pondered the situation. She finally came with us because she wanted to see the movie—*2001: A Space Odyssey*—but she made a point of sitting as far away from Ned as she could get, which was pretty far in that car.

As Elizabeth and I settled into the backseat, Ned turned around and stuck out his hand. "I'm Ned," he said, "nice to meet you." Elizabeth gave his hand a quick shake.

"I'm Elizabeth."

"I know, I know." He threw it into gear and we eased away from the curb.

"So," Ned said, "you both work at the hospital, huh?"

"Yes," Elizabeth said. Tina was quiet.

"That's interesting," said Ned. And that was the end of the conversation.

At one point Ned waited too long before pumping the brakes and we slid under a red light and halfway through an intersection. There were some screeching tires and a few shouted curses, but nobody hit us, and other than that we made it to the theater without incident and without a word spoken by either of the girls. I figured they didn't talk to us because of the car and they didn't talk to each other because they had absolutely nothing in common, except that they both worked at the hospital, a circumstance they obviously weren't interested in exploring. Elizabeth actually seemed a little befuddled, as though she wasn't sure what she was doing there with us.

The movie had a lot of good parts, but it was too long and the ending was vague. Besides the war and the hippies, outer space was the big thing in America; it was the future and we were all supposed to get excited about it. The movie was part of that. It was filled with realistic details about everyday life in space and it also had lots of pseudoreligious stuff in it. The idea was to make us think about the meaning of it all, but all I could think about was being fifty, which was what I'd be in 2001. By the time I got to outer space I'd be an old man, and that didn't seem like such a good thing. I'd probably be too tired to go blasting around in my space suit very much. Fuck it, I thought, I'll stay on earth. Ned and Tina both liked the part with the monkeys best. At first I thought that might bring them together, but Tina was convinced they were real monkeys and Ned thought they were actors dressed up as monkeys and they wound up arguing about it. I made a few comments to Elizabeth during the movie, but she barely responded. At first I thought she was absorbed by the picture, then I realized she was bored; I was looking at her on the sly, studying her face in the light from the screen, when she yawned this huge yawn. Later I caught her sitting there with her eyes closed as if she were meditating or something.

A drive-in burger joint called Johnny's was the hot spot to take a date that summer, but it was all the way out Jefferson Avenue, at least three steep hills beyond the Caddy's range, so after the movie we walked the few blocks to the diner to get something to eat. We had the movie to talk about, so we didn't have to sit there in silence. Tina disagreed with everything Ned said, but at least she was saying something. Elizabeth didn't open her mouth. She just sat there studying the menu as if it were the first one she'd ever seen. The date was more than half over and we hadn't talked to each other at all. From the moment we got in Ned's car, it was like she'd gone off somewhere in her head by herself.

"You didn't like it very much, did you?"

She seemed startled that I had spoken to her.

"Oh no, I liked it a lot." She gave me a kind of half smile.

"I thought maybe you were bored or something. I mean, it did have some boring parts."

"I wasn't bored at all. Really."

"It was kind of long."

"Wasn't that awful," she said, "when HAL the computer sent that poor astronaut flying out into space like that? What a horrible, lonely way to die."

She was right, it was a horrible way to die. And it was one of the best scenes in the movie. It was such a good scene I had turned to see her reaction to it but she wasn't in her seat; she was off on one of her trips to the bathroom.

"Did you see it before or something? The movie, I mean?" It was a question I shouldn't have asked. She looked down at the menu, embarrassed.

"Actually . . ." she said. I felt a hard slap on my back.

"Well shoot my horse! If it ain't Jim Mooney!" It was Texas Billy, all heated up. He put his arm around my shoulders and leaned his face down next to mine; his eyes were red-rimmed and watery, his whiskey breath singed my cheek. "And there's my buddy Ned McCormack." As he stuck out his hand to shake with Ned he grinned at the girls and bowed his head in deference. Tina rolled her eyes with disgust. Elizabeth pulled back in fear.

"How are you, Billy?" I said.

"I'm fine, Jim. I'm fine." He straightened up and stood beside me, his hand on my shoulder for balance. "So you boys are out with the ladies tonight."

"This is Tina," Ned said, gesturing to his date, who was scowling behind a veil of cigarette smoke.

"How do you do, Tina," Billy said, bowing from the waist this time.

"Billy's the one who gave me the car," said Ned.

"Ain't that great," Tina said drily.

Elizabeth had withdrawn into the corner of the booth with her menu. She was staring down at it, her jaw clenched.

"And what is your name, my dear?" asked Billy. With a little shiver she tightened even more. She wouldn't look at Billy. There was a long pause as he waited for her to answer, and then he realized she wasn't going to answer. He smiled the uncomfortable moment away. "Yes, well"—he grabbed my hand and shook it—"okay then, Jim, I'll leave you to your business." An idea hit him and he leaned down to whisper in my ear. "Have you got enough money? Do you need a tenner?"

"I'm all set, Billy. Thanks."

"Are you sure?" He pulled a small roll of bills from his pocket.

"Yeah, really. I'm fine, thanks."

"All right then, I'll be seeing you." He patted me on the back and walked away.

"Who's that bum?" said Tina.

"That's not a bum," Ned answered, "that's Texas Billy. He's a caddy."

"He's a good guy, Elizabeth," I said. "He drinks, but he's really a good guy." She gave me that half smile again; it came from even farther away than the first one had.

"He's got a bullet in his head," Ned said helpfully.

We ate our cheeseburgers in the awkward silence that had become the theme of the evening. The last thing we heard as we were leaving the diner was Billy's laugh; he was sitting at the counter, eating spaghetti and telling stories to the waitress.

I'll say this for Ned: as bad as the date was, he never gave up. He and I had planned to take the girls parking after we ate, and much to the surprise of everyone else in the car, including me, that's exactly what he tried to do.

"Where are we going?" Tina asked when Ned turned onto the old cemetery road.

"I don't know," he said, "I thought we might take a drive."

"I hope you don't think we're going parking." The old cemetery that gave the road its name was a well-known lovers' lane.

"It's such a nice night, you know, maybe we could stop and look at the stars or something."

"You can look at the stars if you want, just take me home first."

Elizabeth suddenly leaned over and whispered in my ear. "I'm sorry, Jim," she said, "but my stomach feels funny all of a sudden. Maybe it was that cheeseburger. Do you think Ned could drop me off first? I really don't feel too good." She grimaced slightly for emphasis.

"No problem," I said.

In spite of her stomachache, Elizabeth perked up considerably as we headed back toward her house. She told me what a nice time she had and apologized for having seen the movie before; she and "a bunch of friends" had gone to see it the first week it was out. Then she told me how busy her life was about to become. Her favorite cousin was coming for a long visit; a family trip to New Orleans was being planned; and she was thinking about taking a couple of courses at an art school in Manhattan. I'd heard about the trip to New Orleans before; the cousin and the art school were news. Obviously, her free time was going to be in short supply.

"What about the hospital?" I asked.

"Daddy said I could quit, as long as I found something else worthwhile to do. That's what the art classes are." I didn't get it. How could hanging around Greenwich Village with a bunch of bohemian hepcats be considered a valid substitute for doing volunteer work in a hospital? Christ, she was liable to wind up posing nude for some bogus Picasso. What was her old man thinking?

"It's the next right, Ned," Elizabeth said, leaning over the front seat and pointing. "Mulberry Court." The date was over and I was pretty sure my new girlfriend was now my former girlfriend. Damn, I thought, I lost her. I had her and I lost her. We were okay as long as she was grounded, I realized, but we couldn't hold up in the real world. We were too different. I was looking out the window to my right and I reached out with my left hand and touched the back of her head. Her hair was soft and fine, like a baby's, almost. I turned and looked at her and she sort of turned her head into my arm and gave me this little smile, this sad kind of smile that gave me hope for just a second and then took it away. We never should have left her yard.

We coasted slow and easy around the corner and

into the cul-de-sac. Ned was pumping the brakes, but they didn't seem to be grabbing too well; I could feel our unchecked momentum in the pit of my stomach. Instead of watching where he was going Ned was staring down through the steering wheel at his wheezing brake pedal. A shiny black Lincoln Continental was parked in front of Elizabeth's house; we were heading right for it, doing about fifteen miles an hour. Elizabeth was happy to be home and unaware of the developing disaster.

"There's Mr. Chapman's car," she said brightly. "He's daddy's boss."

"Hey, Ned," I said, but he didn't hear me. He was too busy pleading with his fickle machine.

"Come on baby come on baby come on baby . . ."

"Hey, Ned!" I yelled.

"Oh no!" Elizabeth cried.

"What the hell!" Tina shouted.

Ned looked up at the last second and yanked the wheel to the right, but it was too late. We hit the Lincoln broadside, dead center, right between the doors. Mr. Brooks's daughter was home.

Ned broke his nose and Tina broke four of her carefully maintained fingernails; Elizabeth and I just got bounced around a bit.

Mr. Chapman turned out to be a short, fat guy with a red face. "Look at that car," he kept saying, "look at that car." I wasn't sure which car he meant.

Elizabeth brought Ned a small towel full of ice cubes and then disappeared into the house without saying good night. Her father stood there with his arms folded across his chest, looking at the cars and slowly shaking his head. Tina went right to work on her nails with a long file she produced from her purse, while Ned sat groaning beside her on the lawn with the towel pressed to his face. Eventually Ned's brother Frank showed up with a tow truck and pulled the vehicles apart. Chapman's car was fine except for the smashed-in doors, but Texas Billy's Cadillac was finished. Tina, Ned, and I squeezed into the cab of the tow truck with Frank. We dropped off Tina, then the car, then we took Ned to the emergency room.

"So," Frank said as he and I waited in the lobby, "you guys have a good time tonight or what?"

I called Elizabeth the next day and the next and the next, but she was never around. It was over, that was obvious. I was a caddy with a broken heart, so naturally I tried to walk it off. I became a super looper. I carried anything Lefty asked me to carry and racked up some serious mileage. I had the respect and the sympathy of my fellow loopers, most of whom had gone through a similar experience at one time or another. Ned's account of the date was an instant hit in the caddy yard, but if I showed up during a discussion of the fiasco they quickly changed the subject.

My courtship of Elizabeth had cut into my earnings—I'd been leaving the course early a couple of times a week to go and hang out at her house—but I quickly made up my losses. The hardest thing about being a super looper was avoiding the card games. I started waiting up top near the bag room between loops so I wouldn't have to hear the familiar sounds of the action—the hoots and curses of the winners and losers, the clink of change being tossed into the pot. I resisted for nearly three weeks. Then, on a slow Thursday afternoon, Adam Brown showed up, ice-cream truck and all. He drove around the putting green and parked right next to the pro shop.

"Hey, Jim," he said, hopping out of the truck, "what's happening?" He was wearing his ice-cream suit—white pants, white shirt, white socks, white sneakers, and a pair of sunglasses. The coin changer on his belt looked full; his pants sagged with the weight of the thing.

I followed him down to the caddy shack, where he was greeted with cheers and slaps on the back from the gamblers. "I'm in," he shouted as he took his place at the table. And sure enough, he punched out the fifty-cent ante as if he were making change for a customer.

"Cool," said Little Petey. "I gotta get one of those."

They were playing blackjack. I stood behind Adam and watched a few hands, excited as always by the speed of the game. With every new deal there was new hope. That was the theme of blackjack, the constant renewal of hope; that was the genius of it.

"What do you think?" Adam said, leaning back to show me his cards. He had a pair of fives. Little Petey, dealing as usual, had a queen showing.

"Double down," I said, "I smell an ace." I was right. And I was in.

"All right," Little Petey said as he flicked out the next hand, "Mooney's back."

For the next few hours I didn't think about Elizabeth at all; I just played cards. My luck was no better than it had ever been, but I didn't care. I lost money, but I lost it slowly and I had a good time in the process. Somebody asked Adam for some ice cream. He said sure and handed over the keys. We couldn't eat it all, but we tried. Clarabelles, Popsicles, Creamsicles, Fudgsicles, ice-cream cones, Italian ices—we passed the boxes around like trays of hors d'oeuvres. The members' kids down at the pool heard about the truck and came trooping up for their share. When it was over there was ice cream everywhere, melting into sticky rivers of orange, purple, chocolate, and pure, sweet vanilla white. Dozens of those little wooden sticks were scattered across the ground. The empty truck sat there at the top of the caddy yard with the freezer doors hanging open as though it had exploded. We were sated, and our benefactor played on, bent over his cards in his white suit, his career as an ice-cream man at a glorious end.

The afternoon wore on, and something quite rare happened—nobody left. The sun burned down behind the hills to the west; the gray summer twilight gave way to the soft dark of summer evening; the cool summer night floated in, full of stars and crickets; and the caddies stayed on in the caddy yard. There was no plan, there was no reason, we just hung around. The card game was the engine; it ran on and on, the intensity rising and falling, the personnel changing. We played in the light of a single overhead bulb and the caddy shack took on the feel of a cabin in the woods. Outside, in the caddy yard, Matt, Texas Billy, Red Ryder, Dolan, and some other non-card players sat smoking and talking in the moonlight. Matt made a run to the liquor store and returned with three cases of beer and a bottle of whiskey. Lefty himself, the boss, joined us for drink and sat in for a couple of hands.

The card game ended and still we stayed, talking and drinking. There was no specific rule about the caddies hanging around the caddy yard after dark, but we assumed it wasn't something the members would be too thrilled about, so we kept it quiet. Eventually the time came for Ned to tell the story of the date. He looked to me for the okay and I nodded my assent. Of course, Ned had improved the tale somewhat. Among other things, he had Chapman in his car when we rammed it and Tina punching him in his broken nose moments after the collision. When Ned got to the incredible-but-true punch line —Tina and Frank had hit it off immediately that night and were now inseparable—the caddies cracked up right on cue. All except for me and Matt, that is. After the disaster, Matt had tried a couple of times to get me to talk about Elizabeth, but I'd vagued out on him. Now, as the others laughed around us, I looked over and caught him watching me. I tried to smile, but it didn't quite work. Then he did a thing the old man used to do; he gave me this quick wink, real quick, that no one else could possibly have seen. It was a signal, just for me, flashed in an instant across the great gulf of that bad moment, a message from brother to brother: I'm with you.

"Goddamn women," Texas Billy exclaimed. "No man ever tried harder than me to understand the mysteries of the female mind, and no man ever failed more completely. Did I ever tell you about my first wife, Charity?" He took a slug from the whiskey bottle. "That was her name, Charity Ann Ford, but she was a terror, a terrifying person. She had this look, the coldest look you ever saw. Ice cold! Colder than ice! She gave it to me at the altar, but I was drunk and I didn't care. Then she gave it to me again, the night she tried to kill me." He took another drink. "Look here," he said. He stood up and unbuttoned his shirt. He pulled it off his shoulders and leaned down in front of Dolan, who pulled back, overwhelmed by the sight. "See that scar there? That's from Charity. She stabbed me while I was asleep. Can you imagine that? I was sleeping on the couch and she snuck up on me and stabbed me with a butcher knife. Let me tell you, it's a hell of a way to wake up." Billy turned so everybody could get a look at the scar. "I jumped up, and she jumped back. 'Jesus, woman,' I yelled, 'what have you done?' And she gives me that look, that cold look, and she says, 'That'll learn ya.' 'Learn me,' I says. 'Learn me what? How to die?'" I moved closer for a better look. It was the same scar he had showed me and Matt that night in his room, the one he said he got from a Japanese bayonet. Billy laughed. "She married a sailor next," he said, "and I heard she stabbed him, too."

10

"How far is that pin, caddy?"

"Too far, sir."

"How far'd you say?"

"Too far, sir. I said too far."

"Too far? What do you mean too far?"

"I mean too far for your sorry ass to ever reach with a cannon, sir, never mind with that fucking four iron you're holding, sir."

"That's what I thought you said, you little shit. What's the rate these days, anyway? Have you got change of a dollar, boy? Never mind. Here you go, son, have another beer. Say, aren't you the one who killed Frank Woods? Why, you little fucker you."

"Yes I am, and fuck you very kindly, sir."

We were just off the eleventh green, me, Matt, and the Ryan brothers, and we were halfway through a case of beer. It was a beautiful night and we were preparing for a key summer event, a splash party for the members' kids at the Colonial Valley pool. We could see the lights and hear the music in the distance. Soon we would be drunk enough to make an appearance. Elizabeth was going to be there. I'd finally gotten through to her on the phone and she had mentioned the party during our brief, remarkably flat conversation. I had hoped her natural verbosity would keep her on the line long enough for me to figure out a way to tell her I missed her, but it didn't happen. I knew it was going to hurt to see her, but I hadn't seen her in nearly a month and I'd reached the point where I could hardly believe we'd ever been together at all.

Technically, Matt and I were to be the guests of the Ryan brothers, a fact that Kevin found particularly amusing. "And finally," he said as we drank, "this social note. The Mooney brothers were seen dancing late into the night at the fabulous Colonial Valley Country Club. Young Jim was spotted trying to grind his way back into the good graces of old flame Elizabeth Brooks, while big brother Matt created a bit of a stir when he spent the evening sniffing around the recently separated and very hot Mrs. Sean Butterworth."

"Hey, asshole," said Matt.

"What?" Kevin protested. "Do you deny that you two are an item around here? Shit, man, you caddy for her about four times a week."

Actually, he was right. Rather than cut back on her time around the course after moving out of Sean's house, Mary had gone the other way. She was playing more golf than ever, and Matt was still giving her lessons.

"She's got her own life," said Matt. "She can do what she wants. She's been a member here since she was a kid."

"Absolutely," Kevin said. "And you'll be pleased to know that one of the things she wants to do is be a chaperone tonight. Or perhaps you already know that."

"As a matter of fact, I do."

"I'll bet you do, you dog."

"Wait a second," Matt said. "Is that the one and only Eddie Floyd I hear?" The blast of horns that kicked off "Knock on Wood," Floyd's hit from a couple of years before, bounced down from the pool. Matt jumped to his feet. "It is indeed," he said, and he started to dance out across the green. We were sitting on a slope just below the green; Matt was above us, silhouetted against a moonlit stand of trees. He sang the song as he danced. His moves were smooth but strong, like the song, and his voice was on the money; it matched up perfectly with the record. "You better knock . . . on wood." He stayed with it all the way, singing every word, right to the end. We applauded when he finished. "Thank you, gentlemen, thank you," he said. Then he shouted in the direction of the pool, "And thank you too, Eddie, you funky man."

We made our way across the course, passing other groups of drinkers as we went. Mary was at the gate with the guest list and she was happy to see us. There were Chinese lanterns strung across the pool and a long paper banner hanging on the fence: Colonial Valley Summer Splash '68. The snack bar was open and there was a huge stereo system set up at one end of the pool. "Sunshine of Your Love" started playing as soon as we walked in; along with my beer load it made for an extremely cool entrance. The place was packed. A few kids were swimming, but most were on dry land trying hard to look cool. It was a crowd of what were called rah-rahs. The males sported lots of white jeans, short-sleeved madras shirts, loafers, and no socks. The females wore madras dresses or sleeveless blouses with either miniskirts or culottes. I had opted for blue jeans, a button-down oxford shirt with the sleeves rolled up, and loafers with socks. It was a reliable look; I'd been wearing the same kind of shirt since kindergarten. There were a few scruffy surfer types present, but there were absolutely no greasers in sight.

I wandered around for a while pretending I was just there to have fun. I danced a few times with girls I didn't know and shot the breeze with the Ryans for a while. Then I got down to the business at hand. It was crowded and dark, but I finally spotted her standing with a group of people by the snack bar. I didn't want to walk right up to her, but I didn't want to stand around and wait for her to spot me either. I decided to sink back into the crowd and wait for a better opportunity to approach her. Then she saw me. She said something to her friends and came over.

"Hi, Jim." She gave me a quick kiss on the cheek.

"Hi, Elizabeth."

"It's good to see you. How have you been?"

"Pretty good, how about you?" She looked great, of course. "How are the art classes going?"

"I decided not to take them. Going into the city twice a week would have been too much."

"I've been by the hospital a few times. I haven't seen you there."

"Oh, I quit the hospital."

"Really? So, what have you been doing?"

"Not much, I guess." A big guy walked up and stood beside her.

"I was looking for you," he said, "where'd you go?"

"Dennis," she said, "this is Jim Mooney. Jim, this is Dennis Sawyer. He goes to Penn State. He plays baseball." We nodded at each other. Dennis was clearly not premed. Could a baseball player possibly be dumber than a football player? I wondered.

"Jim's a caddy," Elizabeth said.

"Oh yeah?" said Dennis. "I didn't know they let caddies come to these things."

"I'm with some friends."

"It's against the rules at our club."

"What is?"

"Caddies coming to parties. Unless they park cars and stuff."

"Yeah, well . . ." Just then Matt walked over. I introduced him. I knew he was curious about Elizabeth, but before he could say anything to her, Dennis spoke up.

"You a caddy too?" he asked. Matt looked at me, I shrugged my shoulders.

"As a matter of fact I am," Matt said. "Why?"

"Just curious. Seems like there's a lot of you guys here tonight."

"Dennis, please," Elizabeth said.

"Oh, is that how it seems?" said Matt.

"Yeah."

"Can I ask you a question?"

"Sure, why not?"

"When you scratch your ass, does it mess up the part in your hair?"

"Hey, man," Dennis said. He balled his fists and took a step toward Matt.

"Just curious," Matt said. "Come on, Jim. Let's find some caddies to talk to. This guy's too sophisticated for us. It was nice meeting you, Elizabeth." Matt left, Dennis glared at him.

"Well," I said, "I'll see you around, Elizabeth." I walked off into the crowd. Suddenly she was beside me. She took my hand and for a moment it was just the two of us, alone in the middle of the party.

"I'm sorry, Jim," she said. She looked like she might cry.

"That's okay," I said. "Forget it."

"You hate me, don't you? I know you do." Christ, she got that wrong.

"No, no I don't." She reached up with her left hand and pushed her hair back behind her ear. To my surprise, it was a familiar gesture; she really was my old girlfriend. I wanted to kiss her. Dennis appeared beside us. "Let's go, Lizbeth," he said.

"I'm sorry," she said to me again. She let go of my hand as Dennis led her away; too bad old Todd wasn't around to fall in the pool so I could save him again.

"That's all right," I said.

I took a walk on the back nine. A good golfer could play at night, I realized, if he had a ball that glowed in the dark and he kept it in the fairway. Except for cheerleading practice and making out in her room, I couldn't remember much about my visits to Elizabeth's house. I could be a night-shift caddy. We must have talked about school or current events or something. I could wear one of those miner's hats with the light on the front. So much for swimming naked together in the ninth-hole lake. "Where'd that ball go, caddy?" "I lost it in the moon, sir."

A few minutes after I got back to the party, Sean showed up. He was very drunk, which was not a good thing, since the final round of the club championship was scheduled for the next morning. Mary tried to ignore him but he was obviously on the verge of yet another big scene, so she left the gate and walked over to the parking lot with him. I drifted over by the fence to watch. They stopped about fifty yards away under a light. Sean did all the talking. I couldn't hear what he was saying, but I could see that he was angry. Mary just stood there, arms across her chest, head down, listening. He ranted away at her for five minutes or so but she never moved. Finally he was done. He stood there staring at her. He was waiting for her to say something, I guess, but still she wouldn't meet his gaze. Suddenly he reached out and grabbed her chin and forced her to look at him. They held that pose a moment, then Mary jerked her head free. She spoke at last, just a word or two, and the second her mouth moved, Sean's arm flashed and I heard the sharp crack of his hand on her cheek. And then a strange thing happened—Mary turned and looked right at me. She must have known I was watching them. I started to look away but she wouldn't let me. Our eyes met and even at that distance, even in the dark like that, I could see the pain she was in and I knew that she wanted me to see it. She continued to look at me, absently rubbing her cheek, then tears filled her eyes and she turned away. Sean spun around and headed up the hill toward the clubhouse. Mary got into her car and drove away.

I found Matt and told him what I'd seen. He took off across the course in the direction of Mary's father's house.

I slept in the next day and let all the time and effort I'd put in to Sean's golf game go to waste. He called the house looking for me and I told my mother to tell him I was sick. I just didn't want to see the son of a bitch. I didn't want to help him win. I didn't want to say "good shot" and "nice putt" to him all day long. I didn't want to smile at him when he made a birdie. I didn't want to shake his hand when it was all over and he was the champ, the hand he slapped his wife with. So I stayed in bed and he lost, three holes down with two to play. Red Ryder caddied for him. "The cocksucker was drunk for the first nine holes," Red later explained, "then he sobered up. Shit, if he'da stayed drunk he might a won." Strange thing was, I felt bad about him losing.

About a week later, on a Monday, I came in from playing golf and found my mother waiting for me in the kitchen. She was sitting at the table with a file folder in front of her.

"What's your brother up to these days?" she asked.

"I don't know, Mom. Same old thing, I guess. Why?"

"Did you play golf with him this morning?"

"No, it was just me and Ned."

"He didn't come by for dinner this week. He wasn't here at all."

"Don't worry about it, Mom. He's fine."

"He's avoiding me." She tapped the folder; it was bulging with documents. "He knows about these, doesn't he?"

"Yeah, sort of." My mother had spent a good part of the summer pulling together Matt's transcripts and compiling a list of schools that might accept him. She sent away for applications and then filled them out herself. She even wrote the necessary essays, which were all neatly typed. She had tried to keep it a secret at first, but when the stuff started coming in the mail we all realized what she was doing. Matt was bugged when I told him about it, but he never said anything to her.

"Well, they're ready now, but I'm not going to sign them. He's got to do that himself."

"I think you better sign 'em, Mom. He won't want to do it."

"No. He has to accept some responsibility, Jim. He knows this is the best thing for him."

My mother was eighteen when World War II started and twenty-two when it ended. She spent those years in New York City, where she was born and where she lived until she married my father. She worked as a bookkeeper and went dancing at the USO. Quite a few of the boys from her neighborhood were in the service and she wrote to them and worried about them and said prayers and lit candles for them in St. Patrick's Cathedral. She also wrote to my father—they had met as kids while she was visiting some cousins who lived next door to him—and worried about him and prayed for him, and he made it through. A lot of the boys she knew made it through, but not all of them. Some of them died in spite of her letters and prayers. Her best friend's brother died on an aircraft carrier in the Pacific. A week after she learned of his death, my mother went to the movies. Suddenly she found herself watching newsreel footage of a kamikaze attack on an aircraft carrier. It was his aircraft carrier; it was the battle he died in. She saw the chunky Japanese planes screaming low across the sky. She saw terrible explosions. She saw balls of flame roll across the deck; thick black smoke rise from the twisted wreckage; antiaircraft fire stream into the air. She saw dead and wounded sailors. She waited in dread for the sight of a familiar face but was spared that horrible detail. She never cried or anything when she used to tell us the story. It was sad and awful, but that wasn't her point. Her point was: that's what life was like then; that's what could happen.

"I'm going over to Matt's place," she said, standing up. "Why don't you come with me?"

"He may not be there."

"Then we'll wait for him."

Mrs. Henry let us in and we sat in his room for over an hour.

"We could be here forever, Mom," I said.

"Where could he be?" She was sitting on his bed, holding the folder in her lap.

"I don't know. Why don't you just sign them and get it over with?" She hesitated, then took out a pen and wrote a short note on the front of the folder. She placed the folder on Matt's pillow.

"I'll leave them here," she said.

"Great, let's go."

We were halfway down the block when she changed her mind and sent me back for the folder. She signed the applications right there, leaning on the hood of a car, then we walked uptown and mailed them from the post office. Then we went to the five-and-ten and had ice-cream sodas.

Sean had disappeared after losing the club championship. For two mellow weeks he was nowhere to be seen. The rumor was he was living with his girlfriend in New York. Then, as suddenly as he disappeared, he was back. It was late on a Sunday afternoon. Matt and I were in the same loop, caddying for two older couples. Sean's GTO came racing down the road and up the hill to the clubhouse. A few minutes later we saw him running out onto the course in our direction.

"Look at this asshole," Matt said as Sean came toward us.

A second later he was on us. He charged up to Matt and stuck a finger in his face; Matt didn't flinch.

"You stay away from my wife," Sean barked. One of our frightened golfers tried to protest, but Sean cut him off.

"Shut the fuck up," he said, then he turned back to Matt. "I'm warning you, motherfucker. Stay the fuck away from her or I'll kill you."

And that was it. He turned and walked off the course. A few minutes later his car came speeding down the hill, tires squealing as he made the turn, and disappeared up the road. I was scared, but Matt didn't seem worried at all. "What a fucking hard-on," was his only comment.

When I got home that afternoon, the long-lost Rambler was parked in front of the house. A pair of bony, sandal-clad feet were hanging out the window.

11

Matt's roommate, Michael "Where the hell have you been?" Quinn, was one of those guys who are always running late. No matter where Quinn was, he always had to be somewhere else immediately. He was never at his final destination; he was always on the move, just stopping by, just passing through. He had an elaborate schedule of his own creation that he had to stick to, but since no one who knew him expected him to be anywhere he was supposed to be when he was supposed to be there, the schedule was meaningless to everyone but Quinn. Quinn knew this at some level, which was why he was so relaxed in spite of his eternal tardiness and endless running around. For a guy who was always in a hurry, he was incredibly slow. I shook his leg to wake him up.

"Hey, Little Moons," he said as he sat up, "what's happening?"

"Not much, Quinn. What's happening with you?"

"Just dropping off the Rambler. I have to get up to Boston, so I can't stay long. Man, you got tall. Where's your brother?"

"He's got his own place. What's going on in Boston?"

"School, I hope."

"Which one?"

"Don't know yet. Have to find one fast though, or I'll lose my exemption. His own place?"

"Yeah, come on." We drove over in the Rambler, which had the unmistakable tang of home about it; Quinn had been pretty much living in it since May. He was in transition from Catholic college student to hippie and there was something distinctly seedy about him. His hair was getting long, but he was still parting it on the side and he was still wearing black plastic eyeglasses. He was growing a beard, but it wasn't going too well; several small clusters of what looked like pubic hair were scattered about on his long, bony face. The thickest of these was at the point of his chin, and Quinn had developed the less-than-attractive habit of tugging on it. He had the proper clothes—bellbottom jeans, tie-dyed T-shirt, leather sandals with tire treads for soles—and they were appropriately grimy-looking, but he wasn't quite at home in them; he seemed a little self-conscious about the way his pants flapped around his ankles when he walked.

Matt was happy to see Quinn and quickly filled him in on everything that had been happening. Quinn was impressed with Matt's room and even more impressed with the fact that he had an angry husband after him. He was not impressed at all, however, with Matt's willingness to be drafted. The idea horrified him, and he wasn't afraid to say so.

"I don't understand your thinking on this, Moons. You want to go to Vietnam? You want to shoot people? Is that it?"

"I don't want to shoot anybody, Quinn. Don't be so dramatic. I'm talking about experience. I'm talking about what is probably the most interesting place on earth right now."

"Experience? Interesting? Are you out of your fucking mind? The interesting experience is a fucking nightmare, Moons. Don't fuck around with the fucking war, man. Come on up to Boston with me. They got so many schools up there, one of them is bound to take you. And the chicks, man, the place is crawling with hippie chicks."

"Forget it, Quinn, I'm sick of school. How's the Rambler?"

"The Rambler's fine. Don't change the subject. Listen, I know a guy who can show you how to get out on a psycho. Guaranteed. You won't even get to the part where they look up your asshole. They'll think you're so fucking crazy, they'll toss you right out on the street. I got his number right here." Quinn pulled out the fattest wallet I'd ever seen. It was jammed with business cards, cocktail napkins, matchbook covers—there was even a piece of a paper plate with a number scrawled on it.

"Quinn, please. You've only been here half an hour. Relax. We can talk about it later. Are you hungry?"

"Of course I'm hungry."

"Good, let's go to the diner. I'm buying."

"I'm going to find the number and give it to you and I want you to call the guy. Will you do that? Will you at least call him?"

"Quinn . . ."

"Will you do it? Tell me you'll do it or I'll leave right now."

"All right, I'll do it."

Quinn kept talking as we started down the stairs.

"I know you, Moons. You vagued out and got this stupid idea in your head and you let it grow and let it grow and after a while you thought it actually made sense. Well, I'm here to tell you it doesn't make any sense at all."

Matt laughed as Quinn rambled on.

"I don't know what I'd do without you, Quinn. What the fuck's happening with your hair?"

Quinn loved the diner of course, especially our status as regulars; he was unabashedly in awe of Matt's survival skills.

"Man, you really know how to live," he said as he polished off his hot roast-beef sandwich.

"You know me, Quinn," said Matt, "I'm a connoisseur."

"Hey, man," Quinn said, hunching forward, "I just got an idea. Let's go to the beach. I haven't been to the Jersey shore in years." Matt grinned and looked at me.

"There it is, Jim," he said, "Quinn's mind in action. The man's on his way to Boston, which is north, so he wants to go to the shore, which is south." Matt turned his wry smile on Quinn and Quinn smiled right back at him; he was doing the thing he most loved to do, he was changing his plans.

"Fuck Boston," he said. "Boston ain't going anywhere. Come on, man. Let's do it. It'll clear your head out. You may not have noticed, but you ain't been thinking too clear lately."

"I don't know," Matt said. He was looking for a way out.

"What do you think, Jim?" Quinn asked. "You ready for a little beach action?"

"I think it's a good idea, Matt," I said. "We haven't gone anywhere yet and the summer's practically over."

"That's it then," said Quinn. "The Mooney boys are clearly in need of a change of scenery. The work is done, it's time for fun." He stuck his arm up in the air. "Check, please," he said with the authority of a diner veteran.

After a summer under Quinn's care, the Rambler was not quite in great shape. It wouldn't do more than fifty and we had to stop and add a quart of oil every sixty miles or so, but the radio worked and so did the brakes, so fuck it, what did we care? We cruised down the parkway with the windows wide open, Matt and Quinn in the front, me and a cooler full of beer in the back. The farther from town we got the happier I felt. I was sick and tired of everybody and everything, but I didn't know it until I got away. I could feel the weight lifting as the exits ticked by. I drank beer after beer, exhilarated, and got drunk right there in the backseat.

"God, I feel good!" I yelled. Quinn turned around to look at me.

"You're drunk," he said. "Good for you."

"Hey, Quinn," I said, "do you realize what we're doing?" The late-afternoon sun had turned the inside of the car to gold. I was full of joy and revelations.

"No. What are we doing?"

"We are taking a vacation."

"Is that right?"

"Yes, that's right. You, me, and Matt. We are on our fucking vacation. Right this minute. As we speak."

"As we speak?"

"That's right."

"Outa sight," Quinn said. "But I have a question."

"What's that?"

"What are we on vacation *from*?"

"From our fucking jobs, of course."

"But I don't have a job," he said. He thought he had me, but I had him.

"Well then, Quinn," I said, "you'll have to be on vacation from not having a job. How's that sound?"

"That sounds perfect, Jim. Just perfect. Gimme a beer."

I fell asleep, and when I awoke it was dark and I was alone. The Rambler was parked on a narrow but busy street; a line of cars filled the block, radios blasting, horns blowing, and a steady stream of passersby flowed past on the sidewalk. I sniffed the air and knew instantly where I was—Seaside Heights, where the Atlantic Ocean meets the sausage sandwich. I joined the crowd and followed the noise and the lights out to the boardwalk, an elaborate arrangement of neon, wood, grease, and cheap stuffed animals perched in the ancient sands of North America and dedicated to the pursuit of such brainless pleasures as having someone try to guess your weight. The American family was out in force; thousands of sunburned dads, tired moms, sullen teenagers, bratty ten-year-olds, and crying babies were drifting up and down the splintery promenade, hanging loose and trying to have fun. I scarfed up a couple of slices of infra-red pizza and headed for the nearest cigarette wheel. You could win anything, from a rabbit-foot key chain to a color television at the dozens of wheel-of-chance booths that lined the Seaside boardwalk, but cigarettes were by far the most popular prize available. It was the deal of the century; if your number hit, you got a carton of smokes for just a dime. I invested a half dollar and won on my first spin.

I strolled along, enjoying my vacation, at ease in the honky-tonk night. The barkers barked at me and I obeyed them. I played the wheels again and won a cigarette lighter and a fresh copy of *Sgt. Pepper*. I blasted a paper target to bits with a pellet gun that was chained to the counter of the shooting gallery. I shot baskets and won a large hot-pink elephant that I quickly abandoned on a bench. I ate a basket of fried clams. I watched people slam each other around on the bumper cars, then joined them and got slammed around some myself. I ate a twelve-inch-high ice-cream cone. I tried my best to win the water-gun horse race but lost to a little kid wearing a felt hat with a giant feather sticking out of it and his name stitched on the brim. I ate a piece of red licorice three feet long. And every so often I stepped to the railing and stared out in the direction of the ocean. The Seaside boardwalk was not a place to contemplate the power and majesty of the sea—once your eyes adjusted you could just barely make out the pale foam of the shore break one hundred and fifty yards away—but you could hear it, and when the wind shifted you could smell it as well; the sharp salt air cut right through the heavy odor of the grills and deep-fryers.

I found Matt and Quinn in a crowded little tavern down near the end of the boardwalk. I spotted them through the screen door, leaning on the corner of the bar. It was a casual reunion; I'd never doubted that we'd hook up eventually that night and neither had they. There was something so right about the trip that routine planning wasn't necessary. In fact, we were so completely in sync that I didn't even blink when Matt slipped me his fake ID as I stepped up beside him. I just handed it over to the bartender as if the whole business bored me. He glanced at it, equally bored, wiped the bar in front of me and asked me what I wanted. The next thing I knew I was having my first-ever beer in a bar. We were humming now. I took a sip, my stomach fluttering. "Not bad," I said. Matt laughed out loud and slapped me on the back. Quinn quickly ordered another round.

It was a real family kind of place; husbands and wives drank together while the kids streamed in and out, cadging Cokes and hitting up their parents for money. The jukebox, cranked all the way up, mixed the Top Forty together with Elvis, Sinatra, Nat King Cole, and even some Big Band stuff. We kept to ourselves—we were the youngest ones in there—but we were next to the cigarette machine so we made at least nodding acquaintance with everyone because everyone smoked. It was a friendly crowd, feverish but relaxed. They were hardworking folks working hard to have fun and trying hard not to hear the clock ticking away their precious two weeks of leisure. People get unbelievably drunk in a beach bar in the summer, I discovered, unbelievably drunk and unbelievably loud. No work tomorrow! No getting up, no getting dressed, no starting the car, no traffic, no punching in, no boss on your ass all morning, no shitty lunch break, no boss on your ass all afternoon, no punching out, no driving home, no meat loaf for dinner, no going to bed, no tossing and turning, no getting up and doing it all again. Fuck that! You're on vacation, two weeks of doing exactly what you feel like doing. Two weeks in heaven. Two weeks in a little beach cottage surrounded by identical little beach cottages built so close to each other you can hear your neighbors' conversations, not their arguments but their actual conversations, and they can hear yours and so what, who cares? Somebody else was sleeping in your bed last week and somebody else will be sleeping in it when you're gone, but the place is yours for now, you're the temporary king of your temporary castle—two bedrooms, a wood-paneled living room, a small kitchen with a counter and a couple of stools, a screened-in porch, and a cute little front yard no bigger than the trunk of your car with a plaster statue of a dolphin in the middle of it, surrounded by shining blue gravel. You've got seashells for ashtrays and a decorative fishnet on the wall. You've got bathing suits and beach towels drying on the fence. You've got people sleeping everywhere, on every available flat surface. You've got no privacy at all, but you don't care, because you're on vacation, you've got it made. Two weeks at the beach, two weeks in the beach bar.

We drank until closing time and then set off in search of a place to sleep. We got our sleeping bags and stuff out of the car and walked south on the boardwalk about a half mile beyond the commercial section, where it was much darker and much quieter. We picked a spot midway between two streetlights for maximum darkness and crawled under. The boardwalk sat right on the sand at that point, so we had to burrow out a space big enough for the three of us. Sleeping on the beach was against the law, so we piled the sand on the street side so the cops wouldn't see us when they cruised by with their searchlights. It was gritty but cozy. Down there, away from all the rides and attractions and shit, we could hear the waves much better and that timeless rhythm—thump, whoosh, thump, whoosh—put us to sleep fast.

I didn't feel too good when I woke up. First there was a moment of total disorientation, when I had no idea where I was. Then I sat up and hit my head on a beam, which doubled the intensity of what was already a major hangover. Matt and Quinn were better off than I was, but not much. We lay there groaning and farting until finally Matt had enough.

"Fuck this," he said. "I'm going in."

"In where?"

"In the ocean, of course. It's the only cure. Let's go."

"It's too cold. We'll die."

"What are you talking about? It's the end of August."

"But it's six-thirty in the morning."

"Trust me, it'll feel great."

We snaked into our bathing suits and crawled out into the morning light. The sun was just coming up and hanging low over the long horizon. The air was cool, the beach wide and empty. It was low tide and the ocean was flat and calm with just a mild break. The seagulls—"beach pigeons" Quinn called them— were swooping about as always; one flew by with a chunk of pizza crust in its beak.

"There's only one way to do this," Matt said. "You guys ready?"

"No."

"Good. Last one in buys breakfast."

With a shout we took off and raced for the ocean, arms pumping, sand flying. Picking up speed on the downslope, we sprinted across the hard, wet sand and splashed out into the shallows. Just as I started to lose my momentum I leapt and flattened out in a long dive. I hung above the water just a second, then slipped beneath a small, sparkling swell. It wasn't so bad, really. My heart stopped, my balls retracted deep into my body cavity somewhere, and ice picks were driven into my ears. So many things hurt at once I actually screamed underwater, and then my teeth hurt too. Still screaming, I burst to the surface and swam a few quick strokes. I could hear Matt and Quinn yelling as well. I got to my feet, shivering in the waist-deep water. "FUCK THIS!" I shouted. Matt turned and charged in my direction. I tried to run, but he jumped on my back before I could take two steps. "I am the king of the ocean," he cried as he dragged me under. We wrestled like kids and his strength surprised me, as it had always surprised me. Matt was stronger than he looked; after a couple of key fights early on in his career as a kid, he became known as someone not to be messed with and I became known as someone with a big brother who was not to be messed with. He held me up over his head, spun me around, and tossed me into the surf. Then Matt and I attacked Quinn, and five minutes later the three of us were back on the beach, refreshed and ready for inaction.

It was a long, hot, noisy day on the Jersey sand. Armed with only a cooler and a portable radio, we gallantly held our position hour after hour as the sun climbed up and across the burning summer sky. Swim, snooze, swim, snooze, eat, swim, snooze. We were flesh on the beach and nothing more. We baked ourselves like hams—big, briny hams, and sank into such torpor that we could barely remember our names. Besides the crashing of the waves and the blaring dissonance of ten thousand radios, the Seaside cacophony included the metallic screech of the Wild Mouse, the compact little roller coaster that hung out over the beach, and the terrified screams of those foolish enough to ride on the ancient contrivance. The smells were as varied and interesting as the sounds. Suntan lotion, fried onions, hot dogs and hamburgers, perfume, sweat, and, of course, the sea itself combined to create an extraordinary bouquet that grew more pungent as the day wore on. As the crowd swelled around us we had desultory conversations with girls from all over the state.

"What's your name?" Quinn asked one, without even lifting his head from the blanket.

"Maryanne," said Maryanne, a scrawny blonde in a purple bikini. She was carrying a carton of Benson & Hedges, America's hippest new cigarette.

"Do you want to get married, Maryanne?"

"Who to?"

"To me, of course."

"Yeah, right," she said. She looked at Matt. "Your friend's a real comedian. What's your name?"

"Franklin, Franklin Pierce," said Matt.

"Well, me and my friend are down there by the lifeguard stand, Frank." She pointed with her cigarettes.

"Great," said Matt, "we'll stop by. Where are you from?"

"Metuchen. What about you?"

"Los Angeles."

"California?"

"That's the one."

"Get out of here. Really?"

"Sure."

She studied us a moment.

"Then how come you're not tan?"

O Maryanne, we underestimated you.

"Well," said Matt, "actually, we're musicians."

"Like a band?"

"Sort of, yeah."

"What do you mean, 'sort of'?"

"Well, you know how the Monkees don't really play on their records?"

"Yeah? So? Everybody knows that."

"Well, that's us."

"What?"

"We're the guys who do play on their records."

"That's right," Quinn added helpfully. "We're the Monkees, but we're not. We're like the, uh, un-Monkees."

We watched as Maryanne mulled it over: it would be pretty cool if we really were the un-Monkees, but we were probably just a bunch of wiseasses.

"You know what I think?" she finally said.

"What?"

"I think you're full of shit. See ya."

About the middle of the afternoon, as we were lying there half conscious, Quinn started asking Matt about Mary. Matt had been typically vague when he told Quinn the story initially and Quinn wanted the details. He tried to be subtle, but as soon as he brought up the subject I sensed where he was heading and so did Matt. Quinn wanted to know the same thing I wanted to know, the same thing, in fact, that Sean wanted to know. After a few minutes of basic questions about her looks, her background, and how the situation had developed, he got to the point.

"What I want to know is, are you two doing it or not?"

"Quinn, you are so fucking crude."

"Answer the question, Moons."

"It's none of your business, but the answer is no."

"Of course it's my business. The sexual habits of

American women are very much my business. And you're lying."

"Don't piss me off, Quinn. I like the woman, that's all."

"And she likes you. That's why there's nothing wrong with it."

"I said, don't piss me off."

"Come on, Moons, lighten up. I'm your friend, for God's sake. I'm happy for you. An affair with a married woman is a very advanced kind of a thing. Very sophisticated. Hell, I'm proud of you."

"Well, don't be. She's not married, she's separated. And we're not having an affair, we're just friends."

"I wish I had more friends like that."

"Hey, asshole, knock it off."

"Okay, okay, relax."

Quinn stood. "I'm going up for a meatball sandwich. Anybody want to come?"

"Bring me a Popsicle, would you, Quinn? Cherry. You want anything, Jim?"

"I'll have the same."

"Two cherry Popsicles, coming right up."

Quinn headed off across the sand, weaving through the crowd. His narrow back looked pink and blotchy.

"Fucking Quinn," Matt said. "What a piece of work."

We lay there and listened to the radio. The basic AM set, repeated over and over, consisted of "Jumping Jack Flash" by the Rolling Stones, "Hurdy Gurdy Man" by Donovan, "Hello, I Love You" by the Doors, "Mrs. Robinson" by Simon and Garfunkel, and Herb Alpert's fluke hit, "This Guy's in Love with You." Exceptional beach music, it passed the ultimate test; it not only sounded good, but when you listened to it, even though you were flat on your back doing absolutely nothing, you felt you were accomplishing something. Your mind was actually occupied. I couldn't learn rudimentary French, but I knew all the lyrics by heart and when I wasn't actually hearing the damn tunes I was playing them in my head: "'Twas then when the hurdy gurdy man came singing songs of luh-uh-uv. Hurdy gurdy, hurd-ee gurdy, hurdy gurdy gurdy he sa-a-ang." The Beatles were noticeably absent from the lineup that summer, but they were about to drop the big one. When "Hey Jude" arrived in September, the hurdy gurdy man and his friends blew away like feathers.

Quinn's blunt questioning of Matt intrigued me, but it also bugged me. I wanted to know what was going on, but I was trying to forget about all that shit too. I propped myself up on my elbows and slowly scanned the beach. I needed a girl to look at. Then Matt spoke.

"We are, you know."

I looked at him. He was on his back, his hands clasped behind his head. He was wearing a pair of cheap wraparound sunglasses.

"Mary and I. We're lovers."

Quinn was right, it was sophisticated. I'd read the word in books but I'd never heard anyone say it, certainly not the way Matt said it. Christ. Talk about good grammar, my brother knew the correct usage of the word "lovers." I looked out at the ocean. I couldn't think of anything to say. I tried to get a picture of Matt and Mary in my head, but I couldn't.

I couldn't see Sean or the golf course or anything. All I could see was what was right in front of me. Just the ocean and the crowd and me and Matt there on the beach. That was all, nothing else. We were in one world and the other stuff was in another world. All of a sudden I wanted to stay right there. More than anything else I wanted to stay right there on the beach forever. Just keep the radios playing and the waves crashing and the sun shining and the gulls swooping overhead, keep it all just like that. Don't change anything, don't go anywhere or do anything or say anything important at all. Don't tell anybody anything. Don't talk about lovers or love affairs or husbands or wives. Don't tell your brother a thing. Just hand him a beer and point out a girl with nice tits. Don't say a word.

"It's a good thing, Jim. It really is."

I wanted to know, and as soon as I knew, I didn't want to know.

"What about Sean?"

"He's history."

"He's dangerous, Matt."

"Don't worry about him. He's moving to the city."

"Who says?"

"He told Mary. They're getting a divorce."

"He's crazy. He said he was going to kill you."

"That's the way he talks, Jim. He's an asshole, but he's not going to kill anybody."

Matt sat up and took off his sunglasses.

"Hey," he said, "I'm not worried, so don't you worry. Come on, let's take a walk."

They had done it about five times, so far. The first time was the night of the slap. They did it in her room at her father's house, in her big four-poster bed. They'd spent most of the summer just kidding around. She wouldn't talk about Sean or her marriage at all, not even when she moved out. When they did get serious, it was about the draft and the war and Matt's future. She wanted him to go back to school. That was a big thing with her. Of course, as time passed they realized people were talking about them, but so what? That was one of the things they kidded around about. And that's all there was to it, really. They were friends and they kidded around and kidded around and around and around, right up to the moment when they stopped kidding around and became lovers.

"It just happened, Jim. I got to her house that night and she was on the porch, having a drink. Her cheek was swollen from the slap and she was holding the glass against it. Her old man was out of town. She was in a strange mood, I could feel it right away. She wasn't angry, she wasn't crying, she was just . . . finished. You know? With Sean, I guess. I don't know, I was expecting her to be upset, but there was something completely together about her. She sort of turned the tables on me, you know? I went over there to take care of her, but she'd already taken care of herself. It was done. I didn't say anything and neither did she. She was on that swing, that big porch swing, and I sat down next to her and she just reached out and put her hand on my back and said my name and that was it, everything changed. God, it was a beautiful night. I mean the night, the actual night. The porch, the trees, the stars, the fucking crickets."

A lifeguard jumped down from his chair and charged past us and into the surf. He cut through the breakers with quick, powerful strokes. Thirty yards out, a swimmer was struggling to stay afloat and the lifeguard reached him just as he slipped below the surface. He brought the man back to the beach and laid him in the sand. The victim was conscious but exhausted. He was wearing a pair of full-length jeans that must have weighed twenty-five pounds; they were coated with sand and the waistband cut into his big white belly like a noose. He had a thick black goatee and his arms were covered with tattoos. He was pure Seaside, an urban tough guy out of his element.

"Without a doubt," said Matt, "we are witnessing the least cool moment of this guy's life."

Mary told him that when they were together, making love, they were the only two people on earth and nothing else mattered except how good they felt and how happy they were right then at that moment. Nothing else. Two people alone in the world, alone in the universe, alone in a big house overlooking the fifteenth fairway.

"Sex is imagination, Jim. That's all I can say. I always thought it was a physical thing. But it's not. It's all in your head."

Mary told him that once two people made love they were together forever, one way or another, no matter what, and they'd always be connected, no matter what. They'd always have those moments when they were the only two people on earth and nothing could ever change that because that was something just the two of them had shared and it was theirs forever.

"Candles and classical music, Jim. And a real bed, with clean sheets."

Mary told him she liked the way he kissed her, the way he held her head in his hands when he kissed her, and the way he grabbed her behind her knee sometimes and held her just so, and the way he held her hips, the way his thumbs felt against her hips, those two points of strength on her hips.

"We talk about it, Jim, while we're doing it. It's incredible."

Mary told him she liked to watch him sleep, his peaceful face in the moonlight, this person in her bed, this young man. She liked to rest her head on his chest and listen to his heartbeat.

"Goddamn, Jim. Can you believe it?"

Mary told him not to think about anything. After telling him over and over that he had to think about his future, that he had to go back to school, that he had to stay out of the war, she took him up to her room and closed the door and told him not to think about anything at all, except this and this and this.

"You're the only one who knows, Jim. I would have told you sooner, but, well, anyway, now you know."

A small plane flew by pulling a sign—TAN DON'T BURN GET A COPPERTONE TAN. I could never figure out how they landed the damn things.

"So, what do you think?" said Matt.

"I don't know. It sounds pretty serious."

"Well, it is. But it isn't. We're trying to be cool about it, you know, and just let it happen."

"But are you in love with her?" I couldn't imagine how you could sleep with Mary Butterworth and not be in love with her.

"We're just together. Right now, we're together. That's all."

"Sounds like hippie stuff to me. But she's no hippie, and neither are you."

Matt chuckled.

"Believe me, Jim, this is way beyond hippie stuff. This is strictly grown-up stuff."

"So where does it go, then? It's not like she's some chick you're going out with for the summer or something."

"I don't know where it goes. It doesn't go anywhere. Or maybe it does. I don't know. We'll just have to wait and see."

He was making either perfect sense or no sense at all. I didn't know which and neither did he.

"So," I said, "if you marry her, does that mean you quit looping or what?"

"No way," he said. "Looping is my life. I'll never give it up. Hey, how about the size of this fucking sand trap?"

Quinn was waiting for us when we got back, looking hip in his brand-new Monkees T-shirt.

"I'm sorry, men, but I had to eat your Popsicles. How do you like the shirt?"

We did the boardwalk again that night, and with my new sunburn I felt right at home. We even rode on the Wild Mouse. Built out on the far end of a long pier, the bone-jarring old ride featured lurching right-angle turns that hurled you out over the water and made you believe, for one long, exquisite second, that you were about to plunge right off the tracks and down into the black swells surging around the greasy pilings sixty feet below. Quinn did not enjoy the experience.

"I can't believe they let them operate this thing," he said afterward. "It's falling apart. Look at it, the whole fucking thing shakes."

"That's part of the fun, Quinn," said Matt. "I say we go again."

"Fuck that. I'm going to win some cigarettes, then I'm going to the bar. See you there."

We played it the same way we had the night before. Matt went in first and I waited half an hour to give the bartender time to forget the name on the ID. To my amazement the little scam worked again. The scene was the same, only noisier; some screaming Yankee fans were watching their favorite team get beat on TV and doing their best to drown out the jukebox. We drank for about an hour and then the baseball game ended. The next thing we saw were the riots taking place outside the Democratic Convention in Chicago.

"Man, look at that," said Quinn. "It's the real thing."

Crowds of cops and protestors charged through the streets. Cops in riot gear hammered people to the ground with nightsticks. Rocks and garbage cans flew through the air. Small fires burned in a dark and dangerous-looking park as people ran among the trees. A police car drove wildly down a sidewalk, its roof lights flashing. A frantic TV reporter shouted his name into the camera—into the bar—then the picture tilted wildly as the cameraman got knocked to the ground. Quinn seemed mesmerized by the violent images.

"This country's fucked," he said quietly.

"TURN THAT SHIT OFF!" shouted one of the patrons, and—*click*—the set was turned off, just like that. Quinn couldn't believe it.

"Hey, bartender," he called out, "I was watching that."

"Sorry, fella," the bartender yelled back, "the ballgame's over."

"There you go," Quinn said to us, shaking his head with disgust. "That's democracy in action. In America you only have to watch what you want to watch. If you don't like what you see, turn the shit off. That's freedom, boys. That's what it's all about."

Quinn ordered three shots of bourbon, and Matt didn't look too thrilled about it.

"I would like to propose a toast," Quinn said, holding the little glass high in the air. "To the next president of the United States, Richard Shithouse Nixon." He tossed the drink back and slammed the glass down on the bar. "GODDAMNIT, I LOVE AMERICA!" he shouted. Several people looked in our direction; Quinn smiled broadly and gave them a little wave.

"Cool it, Quinn," said Matt. "You're not on campus."

"*Au contraire, mon ami.* When you are a student of life, as I am, the world is your campus, as well as your oyster. Bartender, three more shots please." The bartender brought the drinks and offered Quinn a word of advice. "Keep it down, fella, or you and your friends will have to leave."

"Such a warm human being, don't you think?" said Quinn as the bartender headed for the other end of the bar.

A burly young man with a sunburned face and no neck loomed up beside us, an envoy from a nearby table of loyal American drunks.

"You got something against America, pal?"

"Hey, buddy," said Matt, "we're just minding our own business here."

"I love America," said Quinn. "I love everything about it, from sea to shining fucking sea. I even love you, whoever you are."

The guy swung, a sloppy bar swing that glanced harmlessly off the top of Quinn's head. Glasses and beer bottles smashed to the floor. Matt grabbed the guy around the chest and backed against the wall so nobody could jump him from behind. The bartender came over the bar and everybody cursed and shuffled around for a while, but there didn't seem to be much interest in a real fight. Though we were clearly the wronged party, the bartender kicked us out and allowed our adversaries to remain.

"And don't come back, neither," he yelled after us as we headed down the boardwalk.

"Don't worry," Quinn answered, "we shan't."

Early the next morning, having grown tired at last of Seaside Heights and its endless attractions, we headed south for the more natural environs of Long Beach Island, where the bars, liquor stores, and drive-in burger joints were kept a respectful distance from the beach. No cigarette wheels, no Wild Mouse, no boardwalk at all, just dunes and breakers and twenty-foot lifeboats up and down the beach providing ideal shelter for caddies on vacation.

We didn't talk about anything important for the next two days, not the war or politics or Mary Butterworth. We just floated along in the sunshine, drinking beer and perfecting our body-surfing techniques. We discussed our favorite foods, our favorite albums, our favorite female body parts—Quinn was an ass man, something I couldn't understand at all—and other, equally weighty topics. We avoided profundity at every turn and escaped into the trivial details of low-budget beach life, like finding clean public bathrooms and sneaking into private outdoor showers.

Our first night out on that wide, empty beach, Quinn produced a small bag of marijuana.

"I was waiting for the right setting," he said as he rolled a joint. He handed it to Matt, who casually lit it, took a few puffs, and held it out to me.

"You want to try it?"

"I don't know. What do you think?"

"It's no big deal, really. You'll probably like it." I was leery, but Matt's low-key attitude was reassuring, so, fuck it, I tried it. And of course, nothing happened. We finished the joint and I noticed that Matt and Quinn seemed quieter and, when they did speak, goofier.

"Lot of sand on this beach," said Matt.

"You can say that again," Quinn answered.

The second night, though I was skeptical, I tried it again. I didn't cough as much as I had the first time, but after four or five deep drags I still didn't feel anything.

"Well?" said Quinn. We were sitting around a small driftwood fire.

"Forget it, man. I must be immune to the stuff or something. Hey, Matt, throw me a beer."

And as I watched Matt reach into the cooler, it hit me. He tossed me a can of beer and I caught it with one hand. It wasn't slow motion, it was more like stop action. I saw the beer in Matt's hand, I saw it in midair, and I saw it in my hand. I was vibrating. I could feel myself in space, occupying space, displacing air, my weight leaving indentations in the sand. I was a physical presence in space as I had never been before, existing independent of all other objects, aware of all other objects and of the spaces separating them from me and from each other. I was stoned out of my head.

I was staring up at the sky, thinking about the fact that when you look at the stars you are also looking at the spaces between the stars, when Quinn's face floated in front of me. He was grinning a peaceful, knowing little grin.

"You made it," he said.

I looked at him for just a moment, then I wanted him to float away, and he did.

"Hey, Jim," said Matt, "here's to you." He raised his beer in a toast and I raised mine. We reached across the fire, tapped cans, and drank. Only my beer wasn't opened yet. So I opened it and took a long drink. It was the best beer I had ever had in my life.

"Good beer," I said. Matt nodded in agreement. My voice sounded strange to me. How peculiar, I thought, hearing yourself speak.

"Very good beer," I said again, listening more closely to myself. The words went out of my mouth, around the side of my head and into my ears. I began to understand why talking to yourself was considered crazy.

"Very, very good beer," Matt answered. "Very cold beer."

Suddenly I heard the extraordinary sound of the waves pounding on the sand. I stood up without a word and walked off toward the ocean. I stopped halfway and looked back. Matt and Quinn, with the fire between them, seemed to be floating above the ground in an orange bubble of light. The fire itself looked like a small rocket burning in the darkness, holding the bubble off the ground, just a few feet above the sand. The floating bubble of light looked safe and warm. I would go back to the hovering beer capsule shortly, but first I had to look at the ocean.

The sea looked wild and dangerous in the moonlight; my stomach tightened with fear at the thought of falling in. I'd gotten closer to the surf than I realized, and if the water that suddenly rushed over my stoned feet had been cold I might have had a heart attack. But the water was warm, silky and warm around my ankles, and I wasn't afraid of the ocean at all, not the good old Atlantic Ocean, not my ocean, not Jim Mooney's ocean, not the ocean I had been swimming in since I was a baby. I stood there with my feet in my ocean and felt the pull of the tide. The moon was doing that, the moon was pulling on my ankles with the ocean. Somewhere on the other side of the ocean some other person was standing as I was, standing in the same ocean as me, standing in their ocean, and the moon was pulling on their ankles too. I tried to think of the names of the other oceans and that's when it occurred to me that there was actually just one big ocean. I stood there on the beach and got a picture of the whole planet in my head and, sure enough, all the oceans were connected. The idea that there were five different oceans was just a lot of convenient, man-made bullshit, I realized. There was only one ocean and when I put my feet in it I connected with everything it touched, namely the whole fucking planet.

Quinn appeared at my side while the revelation was upon me. He handed me a lit joint.

"All the oceans are one ocean," I said. I took a deep drag and waited for Quinn's response, which was slow in coming. He looked out at the ocean for a long time and then began to slowly nod his head. He did that for what seemed like ten minutes. Finally he turned to me.

"You can say that again."

We headed home the next day, the Friday before Labor Day. We were tired and mellow and barely spoke a word during the trip. As our exit drew near, Quinn began to pull his stuff together; he'd be hitching on up to Boston.

"Relax, Quinn," Matt said.

"We're almost there, Moons. I've got to get organized."

"Don't worry about it. Take the Rambler. Jim and I will hitch. It's only twenty miles."

"What?"

"I want you to take the car."

And so I knew for certain that Matt was going to do what I had known all along he would do. He was going to let himself get drafted and sent to Vietnam; giving Quinn the Rambler was the proof. I knew it and Quinn knew it too.

"I don't want the car, man. It's your car. You need it."

"You need it more than I do, Quinn. Hell, I'm a caddy, I walk everywhere I go."

"Give it to Jim, then."

"Jim doesn't want this shitty old smoker. He drives the old man's Cadillac. Ain't that right, Jim?"

"Yeah."

"I don't want your car, Moons."

"Come on, man. Take the fucking thing. For chrissakes, it's a piece of crap anyway. It's not like I'm giving you something good."

"I got a better idea. Come to Boston with me. We'll pahk the fucking cah in Hahvad fucking yahd."

"Can't make it."

Matt pulled to the side of the highway and stopped.

"Let's go, Jim," he said. He tossed the car keys in Quinn's lap. "She means the world to me, Quinn. Take good care of her."

"You're a real asshole, Mooney."

"I know."

Quinn pulled a piece of paper from his pocket and handed it to Matt.

"Here's the number of the guy I told you about. His name's Frank."

"Okay," Matt said.

"You told me you'd call him, so don't forget."

"I won't."

"He's a good guy. He'll help you out."

"Okay."

We stood there with the traffic zooming past at seventy miles an hour and said goodbye. Quinn patted me on the shoulder as he shook my hand.

"I'll call you when I'm settled, Jim. You can come up and check out Boston."

"Sounds good, Quinn."

"All right, then. It's a plan, a definite plan."

He turned to face Matt. They were suddenly awkward with each other, unsure even how to get close enough to shake hands.

"It looks like another roadside farewell, Moons."

"Indeed it does, Quinn, and not the last one, I'm sure."

Quinn took a step forward and grabbed Matt's hand. He looked him right in the eye.

"You keep your fucking head down."

"You too."

"I mean it."

Matt nodded.

"I will."

They hugged quickly, then Quinn hopped into the Rambler. He started it up and put it in gear.

"I'm gone," he shouted and pulled away. As he rattled down the shoulder of the road, building up speed to enter the flow of cars, he stuck his arm out the window and flashed us the peace sign. Then the skinny white arm and the old black Rambler disappeared in the river of traffic.

12

I arrived home at dinnertime and knew immediately that something was wrong. Friday night, especially in the summer, was always the most relaxed night of the week. Even if my father had a meeting to go to, he was usually in a good mood on Friday. He'd sit in the kitchen and talk to my mother while she prepared dinner. He'd have a couple of extra beers, or they might share a bottle of wine. If you had a new joke, Friday night was a good time to tell it. On Friday, since we didn't have to worry about homework, we'd stick around the table longer than usual after dinner; my parents might talk about the old days or make some family plans or suddenly decide to take us to the drive-in or to play miniature golf. In the summer it was still light out at dinnertime and with the doors and windows open we could hear the sound of our friends playing in the street. I was excited to be getting home from the beach at that hour because I knew everybody would be glad to see me and they'd want to know all about the trip. But when I came into the kitchen, they were eating in silence and there was something in the air, something awful. My mother and father were more than serious, they were grave. The kids looked upset and confused.

"Where's Matt?" my father asked.

"He went to his place. Why? What's wrong?"

"He got a letter from the draft board. He has to report for his physical."

So it had come at last, the inevitable bad news, the worst news possible.

"When did it get here? Where is it?"

"Today. It's on the mantelpiece."

It was a creepy-looking envelope. The Selective Service System was such a horseshit euphemism. What the fuck did it mean? The three words refused to work together; they stood apart from each other and failed at the basic task of all words—to deliver information. They made as much sense read backward as forward, which was no sense at all. System Service Selective Service System Selective System Service. The letter itself was a different story. It was blunt, and shocking in its bluntness. It told Matthew George Mooney where to be and when to be there. No wonder my parents were so upset. It was a disturbing piece of paper, a deadly piece of paper, and I wondered if it would shock Matt. The war had finally arrived, for real. I called the rooming house, but he wasn't around. Mrs. Henry said he'd come in, taken a shower, and gone right out again.

"Eat something, Jim," the old man said, "then go

find him. The carnival's this weekend, he might have gone there. Take the Cadillac."

I checked the diner first and missed him by half an hour. He had probably gone to see Mary, but there was no way I was going to follow him to her father's house. So I drove over to the carnival. What the hell, maybe he'd take Mary there for their first official date.

Labor Day weekend was a big deal in town. They held a parade, a swim meet, a track meet, softball tournaments, concerts, and put on a big fireworks display. But the main event was a big, noisy carnival that was held each year in a wooded park on the west end of town. Hamilton Park, named for Alexander Hamilton, was the oldest and by far the biggest park in town. Surrounded by steep, tree-covered hills, it included two ponds, known as the first pond and the second pond, the main municipal swimming pool, three adjoining baseball fields, and acres of picnic grounds that featured old-fashioned wooden pavilions and huge fieldstone fireplaces.

The carnival, sort of a Seaside without the sea, was spread out across the baseball fields. There was a Ferris wheel and a dozen or so other rides, all lit up with colored lights. There was a Great White Way, a funhouse, death-defying motorcycle riders riding on the Wall of Death, a Wild West rodeo show, and more. There was even a tent filled with some of "Mother Nature's Mistakes." These weren't human beings—the town fathers wouldn't allow that—they were mostly farm animals and a few snakes and a surprising number of them had two heads, apparently one of Mother Nature's most common mistakes. The star of the show was a two-headed calf that was alive the first time I saw it but had since died and been stuffed. It wasn't as disturbing dead as it had been alive, but it was still pretty hard to look at.

Naturally, I ran into Billy first thing. He was half drunk and feeling good. His hair was conked even higher than usual and he was wearing his best cowboy shirt and boots. He hadn't seen Matt, but he was happy to help me look for him. We covered the whole place twice in less than an hour and Billy rattled on the entire time. He had worked in carnivals, of course, and knew everything there was to know about them, from Ferris-wheel mechanics to the carny vocabulary. " 'Hey Rube!' is what you yell when you need help," he explained. "Brings the other carnies running." We ended up near the makeshift corral where they kept the rodeo horses. I'd noticed the cowboys earlier, hanging around the front of their trailer. They were surly-looking bastards, rolling cigarettes, drinking beer, and working on some of the local girls.

"Well, look here," Billy said, approaching the snow fence holding the animals, "we got some horses all saddled up and ready to go. Say, Jim, did I ever tell you about my cowboy days up in Wyoming after the war?" Billy clicked his tongue and one of the horses walked over to him. Billy started petting him and looking him over. "It wasn't much of a life, I gotta tell ya. All alone in a shack out on the range. Just me and the cows and my horse, Cloud. Great horse, old Cloud, smarter than I was. That was the longest I ever went without a drink. I was dry for a year. I was in one of my antipeople phases, ya see. Sick of people."

"I'm sorry, Billy," I said. "I don't have time for a story. I've got to find Matt."

"Now hold on there, Jim. You saying I wasn't a cowboy?"

"No. I just don't have the time right now."

"You watch this," he said, and in an instant he was over the fence and up on a horse. I didn't know anything about horses or riding, but I could see right away that, for once, Billy hadn't lied. He knew how to sit on a horse.

"Billy, what the fuck are you doing? Get down off that horse."

He jerked the reins and the horse reared up on its hind legs. Then Billy wheeled it around in a tight circle, galloped across the little corral, and pulled up short of the fence on the other side. A couple of cowboys came running out of their trailer.

"Hey, old man, get off that goddamn horse right now."

"Kiss my green Irish ass," Billy yelled. He reared again, then charged across the corral. Only this time, instead of pulling up short, he leaned forward, gave his horse a kick and they flew up and over the fence.

"Son of a bitch!" one of the cowboys yelled. "That old fuck stole my horse." They ran into the corral, mounted up, and took off after Billy, who'd gone racing off toward the dark end of the park.

Over the course of the next ninety minutes, Texas Billy transformed himself into a legend as he led the angry cowboys and eventually the entire police force on a wild chase around town. The first thing he did was disappear. The cowboys searched the park but there was no sign of the horse thief, so they rode back to the corral to meet with the cops. The carnival crowd had no idea that anything was amiss. Then Billy announced himself; he came riding in at top speed, straight down the center of the midway, hooting and hollering as people screamed and dove out of his path. The cowboys remounted as Billy galloped past the corral. For the next fifteen minutes he rode around the park, cowboys in pursuit, while the crowd rushed back and forth from one end of the carnival to the other, trying to follow the chase. At some point, the town's lone motorcycle cop joined in on his big three-wheeler, and his flashing lights and wailing siren made it easier to track the action across the farther reaches of the park. Then, after one more gallop past the crowd—he looked completely happy and completely out of his mind as he thundered by—Billy disappeared again. For the second time the cowboys returned to the corral without their man. Then a call came in on the police radio; Billy had been spotted in the center of town, riding around the green, jumping park benches and disrupting traffic. For another hour, as the sound of the police sirens shifted from neighborhood to neighborhood, Billy made his famous ride, galloping defiantly through the town, plunging across front lawns and through backyards. Before it was over, gangs of kids on bikes, a pack of barking dogs, and a couple of ambulances joined the chase. Finally, the sirens began to grow louder as Billy headed back toward the carnival; we could see the procession of police cars coming along the ridge, lights flashing. Billy was somewhere below them, racing through the park. Suddenly he charged up out of the swale beside the second pond and into the light, the cowboys close behind him. The crowd cheered as he dashed across the last hundred yards of open ground and into the corral. They continued to cheer as he dismounted and sat right down in the dirt, exhausted.

The first cowboy to reach him yanked him up off the ground and punched him in the face, knocking him flat on his back. He was going to hit him again, but a couple of guys grabbed him. I made it to Billy's side and helped him sit up. He was short of breath and there was a cut over his eye from the cowboy's punch, but he was smiling.

"Hell of a good horse," he gasped.

"Are you all right, Billy?"

"I'm fine."

He looked up at one of the cowboys.

"Hey, cowboy, what's the name of that horse I was riding?"

"Fuck you, rummy," the cowboy said with a sneer.

"Same to ya," Billy answered cheerfully.

The police arrived and placed Billy under arrest. As they hustled him through the crowd to the police car, a couple of people reached out and slapped him on the back.

"Thank you, folks, thank you kindly," Billy said. "I hope you enjoyed the show."

Ten minutes after they took Billy off to jail, Matt showed up. He was drunk and upset. He didn't even give me a chance to tell him about the ride.

"She moved back in with him."

"What?"

"She went back to him," he said, "while we were at the beach." He looked flushed, as if he had a fever, and talked fast. "I called her at her father's place. He said she was out. Then he told me to leave her alone. 'Get on with your life, son,' or some such shit. So I called the other house and she answered. She wouldn't talk. She practically hung up on me. She took the phone off the hook. I've got to go see her. Give me the keys."

"No way. You're drunk."

He grabbed my shirt.

"Give me the fucking keys."

"All right, all right. Calm down. I'll drive you. Where's Sean?"

"I don't know. Probably with his girlfriend. Fuck him. Let's go." I followed Matt across the dusty lot to the Cadillac.

"Maybe you should call her tomorrow," I said. "Maybe she's too tired to talk to you tonight."

"Cut the shit," he said. "Let's get a move on." As we drove away from the park, I looked back at the scene. Nestled in between the hill and the lake, the carnival looked like a strange little town, a manic little village built around a giant turning wheel. Who lives there, I wondered, and why all the lights? Crazy people, of course, with a deep fear of the dark and their own way of dealing with it.

Matt stared quietly out the window as we drove. I turned on the radio and turned it off again quickly when I heard the first notes of the Four Tops' "Bernadette." It was a great song, three minutes of pure pain featuring the anguished shouts of lead singer

Levi Stubbs burning in the fires of desperate love; there's a moment near the end when it sounds as though the song is over, but then the dead air is ripped open like a wound as Stubbs screams out his woman's name in agony. It was the last thing we needed to hear just then.

Matt slammed his fist on the dashboard. "Goddamnit! She told me she was getting a divorce."

I think he was more confused than angry. In spite of his claims to the contrary, he hadn't played it cool at all; he'd fallen hard for Mary Butterworth and convinced himself they had a future together. I couldn't imagine her encouraging the idea, but my imagination had proved inadequate from the start, so maybe she did make plans with Matt. They were lovers, after all.

"She hates that son of a bitch," he said. "I know she does." He was obviously talking to himself; the one thing I knew he didn't want to do was discuss the situation.

"I don't think she hates anybody," I said. He turned to face me, eyes burning.

"What the fuck are you talking about?"

"She doesn't hate people. Not even Sean."

He pointed his finger at me; his hand was shaking.

"You don't know anything about it, so shut the fuck up."

I obliged him, and we rode on in terrible silence. The letter from the draft board was folded in my back pocket; I didn't mention it.

As we came down the road that cut through the middle of the golf course we saw the lights shining in the clubhouse on the hill.

"I'm sorry, Jim," Matt suddenly said. We'd be at Mary's in less than a minute.

"Forget it," I said. "Listen, you want to put this off for a while? Get some beer or something?"

"No, I better talk to her. She's probably panicking, you know. The whole thing is kind of heavy, when you think about it."

"You can say that again."

"The beach trip was a mistake. I shouldn't have left her alone like that. I should have stuck around."

I pulled up in front of the house.

"You don't have to wait," Matt said. He jumped out of the car and hurried across the lawn. I saw him jab at the bell a few times and then knock. Mary finally opened the door. She stood there a moment— it looked like she was trying to send him away—then she stepped back. Matt walked in and she closed the door behind him. I turned off the engine and lit a cigarette.

It was an elegant street; fine old houses on deep, sloping lots sheltered by tall, well-tended trees. You could smell the money and the martinis; ours was surely not the first such scene to be played out there. There were lights on in the windows and stars overhead. It was a perfect night, a perfectly hopeless situation. I knew Sean was no good for Mary; just thinking about that slap in the clubhouse parking lot was enough to startle me all over again. I also knew Matt and Mary would never work it out. It was impossible from every angle. So why were they all tormenting themselves? Why couldn't they just see it for what it was and walk away from it? They were all involved with each other, but it didn't seem as though either couple—Mary and Matt or Mary and Sean—was genuinely and completely in love. If that were the case, I figured, things would have been simpler. The lovers would be together and to hell with the rest of it. But that wasn't what was happening. Or was it? Or was it even possible?

Half an hour went by—could they be fucking?—and then Sean's GTO came growling around the corner and pulled into the driveway. He spotted the Caddy right away and weaved over to me. He was drunk, too. Everybody was drunk, except me.

"Hey, Sean. What's up?" He looked surly. I was truly afraid, for all of us.

"What the fuck are you doing here?" He turned and looked at his house. "Is your brother here?"

"No, he's at the beach. I was just passing by. I was going to drop off your wedge."

"What wedge? What are you talking about?"

"Texas Billy got arrested. You got a cigarette?"

He looked at the house again.

"He's gonna be one sorry motherfucker." He charged across the lawn. I leaned on the horn. Matt opened the door just as Sean arrived and Sean slammed him back into the house.

Some people who witness accidents later describe them as having occurred almost in slow motion; in eerie defiance of the laws of nature, the cars hurtling through the intersection freeze into a series of sequential snapshots before they collide and the event is then recalled in vivid detail. The fight between Matt and Sean was not like that. If anything, it was faster than real life, speeded up, like a nightmarish cartoon. By the time I got to the house the hall was destroyed and they were crashing through the dining room—as they rolled across the table someone kicked the chandelier and set it swinging wildly. It was fast, loud, and frightening. They were locked in an angry embrace, grunting and cursing and swinging blindly at each other. They banged through a set of swinging doors and into the kitchen. Mary and I tried to break them apart but we just bounced off their whirling bodies. Plates, glasses, and a spice rack smashed to the floor; the smell of cinnamon filled the room. A second later they were out on the deck, the screen door knocked from its hinges. Then Sean grabbed Matt low around the legs, picked him up, and ran for the edge of the deck; he was going to throw him over. Matt reached down and grabbed Sean around the shoulders. Mary screamed. Sean couldn't see where he was going and mistimed his charge. They crashed through the railing and sailed off into the dark. Everybody screamed. There was an awful thump when they hit the ground. Then it was quiet. The shattered railing framed the emptiness beyond it.

I heard moaning. I walked to the edge and looked down—two figures lay sprawled on the grass below, both in odd postures. At first I couldn't tell who was who. Then one of them moved slightly. The other was still.

Once you've seen a broken neck you wonder why they don't break more often. The design seems so faulty; the big human head is connected to the much bigger human body by just seven little vertebrae, and all of our critical wiring passes through those few fragile bones. In spite of the muscles that surround it, the neck is a weak point. If you lean your head all the way over to one side and then give it a little push, you'll get the idea; when the angles are right (wrong), remarkably little pressure is required to sever the spinal cord. In Sean's case, however, there was considerable pressure involved. It was exactly sixteen feet from the deck to the spot where they landed. They spun around in the air as they fell and Sean ended up on the bottom. The back of his head hit the ground first and his neck snapped under the combined weight of himself and Matt. Death was instantaneous, the coroner would later declare, due to "high cervical cord compression."

When I got to them Matt was sitting up. He was hunched over and his face was tight with pain. The right side of his body was basically caved in; his right arm was broken along with his collarbone and a few of his ribs. Sean was on his back, his head cocked at an impossible angle. I listened to his heart and felt for a pulse but there was nothing.

"How is he, Jim?" Matt's voice was low; it hurt him to breathe.

"Bad, Matt. As bad as he could be. Shit."

"Is he dead?"

"Yeah, he's dead."

Mary knelt beside me.

"I'm sorry," I said, "I didn't see you there."

She reached out and stroked Sean's cheek.

"I'm sorry, Mary," said Matt. She didn't seem to hear him.

I had opened Sean's shirt and you could see the scar from his war wound and the scar on his neck from the automobile accident. Poor old Sean, all chopped up, had finally died the violent death everybody always figured him for. Mary closed his shirt, lay her head on his chest, and began to weep.

As I looked at Sean I realized how much time we had spent together that summer and how well I'd gotten to know him. I knew his moods, his gestures, his expressions. I knew when he had a fresh haircut. I knew when he had a hangover. If he bought a new golf shirt, I knew it. I'd seen him happy and I'd seen him depressed. And of course I'd seen him angry. I knew Sean and his anger. All it took was something small to kick it off, then the door to some deeper anger would open. That was what he couldn't control; once he got pissed off he couldn't keep it from growing. If the door cracked just a bit, he could never get it shut again, not until some real damage had been done. I knew him, but I never understood him. All those years being the wild guy, making trouble for himself and everybody around him, what was that all about? I hated that kind of chaos. Did he find some kind of strange comfort in scenes that made everyone else uncomfortable? Was that possible? Or maybe he was never comfortable at all and so he didn't want anyone else to be comfortable either. Maybe he liked to upset people because he was upset. Maybe he had to do it; he didn't know how to live in a world that wasn't out of control like he was, so he made trouble wherever he went. Or maybe it wasn't that complicated. Maybe he was just the crazy and dangerous son of a crazy and dangerous time.

Mary and Matt and I sat there with Sean, who had made it out of the jungle only to die in his own backyard. Everything had changed forever for all of us. We were a great tragedy and a great scandal, but right then we were just lost and alone, and amazed, I think, to be so completely lost and so completely alone. The world felt huge and empty around us. I heard Matt draw a sharp breath and it occurred to me that he had never broken a bone in his life. I was the one who did that sort of thing—a wrist, an ankle, and, worst of all, my left leg. Matt was with me for that one. We had gone tobogganing deep in the woods, on a secret hill we knew about, more than a mile from the nearest road. We rode all day, through a frigid afternoon in late January, back in the days when New Jersey had real winters. It got darker and we got tired. "One more," Matt said, and that was all it took. We'd made so many runs, I was trying different things to keep it interesting. The last thing I tried was looking at the sky as we flew down the hill. It was great, flashing among the winter stars like that, the cold wind on my throat, and the tree we hit wasn't even that big, not much bigger, in fact, than the bone that cracked. It hurt like hell, but what I remember more than the pain—who can remember pain?—is the surprise I felt when I tried to stand and fell over in the snow. It was such a strange feeling, lying in the cold like that, with my leg feeling hot around the break. Matt towed me out of there on the toboggan, trudging through the snow like a draft horse.

"We are men of the wilderness," Matt said as he stomped along, and that became our code for months afterward. When our mother told us to clean our room, we told her we could not: "Men of the wilderness never clean their rooms." That was the way to break a bone; that's the way bones were meant to be broken.

When old man Woods died it was noisy and busy, but there in the yard with Sean it was quiet. Except for Mary's soft crying there wasn't a sound. We were enveloped in deep silence and the source and the center of the silence was Sean. We were suspended in the profound stillness of his sudden death. He had disappeared into the night, leaving us and his broken heart behind.

I went in the house and called my father. I kept it short. He got the message. I told him there had been a fight, that Matt and Sean were both hurt, but Sean was worse. I didn't say he was dead, I just said he was hurt. On my way back out I grabbed a quilt from the basement, but then I didn't know whether to cover Sean with it or wrap it around Matt. I actually stopped to think about the problem and I might not have moved again, ever, but Mary came and took it from me. When I got back outside the quilt was over Matt's shoulders.

Mary wasn't crying anymore. She was holding Sean's hand and humming something, I couldn't tell what. If Sean had been truly destined to die violently, then Mary must have known it sooner and known it better than anyone else. She must have been waiting for it all those years, wondering if she would be with him when it happened or if she would merely be informed after the fact by a cop or a priest at the door or a call from her father. There must have been a moment, a bad moment, long before, when she realized her wild boyfriend wasn't merely wild; one day she found out that the boy she loved wasn't a boy at all, he was a man in flames. By then it was too late to get away, she'd gotten used to the heat, and she'd gotten close enough to see that he didn't understand any of it very well himself. Then what could she do? She had to stay. And she did, right to the end. Did she ever hum that song before, without thinking about it, while she was trying not to imagine what it was going to be like when he died? Did she hum that little tune to herself without even hearing it, hum it a few times so she'd be ready?

13

The case was presented to the grand jury. The three of us testified about the events of that night and the circumstances leading up to them and no charges were brought against Matt. Of course it was a great scandal, one of the biggest in the history of the town. Some people even wanted my father to resign from all of his public offices, but he refused to do that. The worst thing, aside from the thing itself, was the depth of my parents' disappointment in us. After all their advice and all their warnings, two of their sons had ended up in a backyard at night with a dead body. They knew that Sean had tried to kill Matt—my mother especially despised him for that, and she hated Mary as well—but even that terrible fact was beside the point. They stood by us in public, they never hesitated in that, but as far as they were concerned, we shouldn't have been anywhere near that house that night.

Matt was inducted and sent to basic training in November. After everything else, his being drafted didn't seem so bad. I got a horrible part-time job working in a drugstore for the winter. I stocked the shelves, swept the floors, made deliveries, and came in routine contact with lots of sick people. The only good part of the job was the easy access to *Playboy* magazine. One night in December I was shoveling snow off the sidewalk in front of the place when Texas Billy came walking by, carrying a big suitcase. I hadn't seen him since the Labor Day carnival.

"Goddamn," I said, "Texas Billy in a snowstorm. I can't believe my fucking eyes."

"Hey, Jim, is that you? Well I'll be. How the hell are you, son?"

He'd gotten ninety days in the county jail for his famous ride. He was fresh out and heading for the bus station. Lefty had sent him money for a ticket to Florida. He was wearing a light jacket and coughing pretty hard, so I took him inside and gave him a free bottle of cough medicine. He took a big swig and fixed me with a serious look.

"I read about what happened with you and Matt."

"You and everybody else in the world."

"That motherfucker tried to kill him, didn't he? He tried to kill your brother."

Billy surprised me. It had never really come out that way in the papers. They all had it as an accident, a fight over a woman and an accident. The old man had ordered me not to talk about that night with anyone, so I just nodded my head.

"I knew it," Billy said, "I knew it. That son of a bitch Butterworth. I never liked him."

If that was true, it was the first time I had heard about it.

"Where's Matt now?"

"He's in the Army. Basic training."

"Good, that's good. Hey, what time is it? My bus is at nine. I don't want to miss it."

"You got half an hour."

I set him up with a few packs of smokes and some candy for the trip. As he was getting ready to go I complimented him one last time on his cowboy skills.

"You know, Billy, the way you ride, maybe you ought to think about going back to Texas and starting a ranch or something."

And Billy, who was feeling good about everything, chose that moment to let me in on a secret.

"Back to Texas? Shit, Jim, I can't go back to Texas."

"Why not?"

"Because," Texas Billy said with a grin, "I never been there. See you later, alligator." And he walked off into the snow.

In the spring I started going to church again, of all things. I was looping at a new course a couple of towns away, in the hills to the west. I bought myself an old VW bug to get there and I used to drive past this old country church and one Sunday morning I stopped to light a candle. It was an impulse; I'd always liked lighting candles because it was about as simple as religion could get. "Here, God, I'm lighting a candle. How are you? See you later." There was a mass going on, six-thirty mass, and it was quiet and there were only a few people in the place, so I stuck around. After that, I made it a regular thing, every Sunday. Then a couple of months after Matt left for the war I was sitting there half asleep when I recognized Mary Butterworth sitting a few pews in front of me. I hadn't seen her since the grand-jury hearing. I surprised myself and waited for her in the vestibule after the service. She was shocked to see me, but she covered it well.

She looked as good as ever, maybe better. We chatted about nothing for a few minutes and then, when there was nothing left to say about the church or the weather, she asked about Matt.

"He's over in Vietnam," I said. "He's been there since April."

"Oh no," she said. "Do you hear from him?"

"Oh yeah, he writes to us all a lot. I think I've got one of his letters in the car, if you'd like to see it."

"Oh, thanks Jim, but I've really got to go."

"There's a picture, too."

Mary sat beside me in the car reading the letter, which was short and simple.

"Dear Jim—Just a quickie before we go out. Thanks for the copy of Moby Dick. *An inspired choice. I haven't read it since ninth grade. Anticipate total escape into nineteenth century whaling scene. Bye-bye jungle, hello Ishmael. Congratulations on Boston U. Smart move avoiding the small but deadly Catholic colleges. A big school will be good for you. Find Quinn, he's up there somewhere. You'll have a fucking ball. We had a little thing yesterday. Lost a guy named Rosario, from New York. Good guy. Big baseball fan. We must go to Yankee Stadium*

when I get home. He and his buddies had a spot in the bleachers there. Hey! I flashed on you in the old man's Caddy, cruising up to your baby's house! A genuine vision it was! And I'm here to say it's gonna be a good summer, brother. Okay, that's it. I said it was going to be quick. Kiss everybody for me and keep your head down. And check out the snap! Love—Matt"

He had gotten into the habit of scrawling quotes from the *Bhagavad Gita* at the bottom of his letters to me, and that one was no exception.

"Of all the world's wonders, which is the most wonderful?"

"That no man, though he sees others dying all around him, believes that he himself will die."

I handed her the snapshot, which was in color. It showed Matt in fatigue pants, bare-chested, standing on a hill. He was holding a golf club, a wood, and peering out over a deep jungle valley that stretched away into the distance. The dirt around him was red and there were sandbags and artillery shells nearby. He was posing as though he had just hit a tee shot. At the bottom of the picture he had printed a caption: "Where'd that ball go, caddy?"

Mary started crying and once she started she couldn't stop. I reached out and she took my hand and held it tight. She sobbed as people walked past us on their way to the next mass.

"He shouldn't be there," she finally said.

"He'll be all right. You know Matt."

"I know Matt," she echoed softly.

We sat in silence, side by side, holding hands. She looked over at me and smiled.

"We've had some time together, haven't we?"

"Pretty crazy, I guess."

She looked out the window at the church.

"Do you pray, Jim, in church?"

"I don't know. Not really. I just sit there, you know, and hope everything turns out all right."

She squeezed my hand.

"Oh, Jim," she said, "wouldn't that be wonderful? If everything were to turn out all right? God, that would be so wonderful."

"It'll happen, sooner or later. It's bound to."

Mary handed me the letter and the picture. I didn't want her to go.

"When you write to Matt, would you tell him you saw me? Tell him I said hello. Just say, 'Mary says hello.' And tell him to take care."

She got out of the car and closed the door. Then she leaned down to give me one last message.

"And tell him that I pray for him."

She stood, then bent down once more and gave me the last message.

"And tell him that I think of him."

I cut school the next day to play golf and when I got home from the course just after noon my father's car was in the driveway. It shouldn't have been there and I knew right away why it was there and my first instinct was to turn around and walk away and keep walking and come back later and maybe the car would be gone. I came in the front door and heard my mother crying upstairs as I expected to. I walked through the house and out the backdoor and there was my father in his shirt and tie down in the yard sitting at the picnic table holding Jack and the twins on his lap, holding all three of them on his lap somehow. And yes, it was a beautiful spring day, a terrible sunny day in June with flowers and birds and blue skies, a perfect day with a big hole in it, a big black hole in it full of smoke and fire, and beyond the smoke and fire there was nothing, nothing at all.

Matt was gone. The last thing he saw was—what? —some piece of jungle or something? The bullet that was part of the war that was part of the time that was part of all wars and all times, Matt's bullet, that one shitty little bullet, flew through the jungle and found his heart. His flak jacket was hanging open and the bullet went right in there, right between the two halves of his flak jacket and through his shirt and through his T-shirt and through his chest and through his heart.

As I stood there crying in the yard, I wanted his life to make sense and I wanted to hear his voice again. But his life made no sense at all to me and though I strained to hear it, the sound of his voice eluded me; it was as if I'd never heard it at all. Matt was gone, dead and gone. He was a Catholic school wiseguy with a smart mouth, a good dancer who liked to read, a super looper with sunburned arms, a dead soldier killed in the war. And what was the point? To leave us there like that, in pain forever, crying forever, missing him forever? Had the fucking universe actually arranged itself for that miserable purpose? It was stupid, it was so fucking stupid and final and done; I couldn't believe the stupid wasteful deed was done.

Matt took the bus to Vietnam. That was the last time I saw him, when he got on the bus that took him to Vietnam. He was wearing his uniform, the one and only time I saw him in the goddamn thing.

"I feel like Elvis in his GI phase," he said as we sat on the bench that day, waiting.

They gave him thirty days' leave after he finished all his training, and when his time was up he put on his uniform and came downstairs early to have breakfast with my parents. He had to report somewhere in Newark and my father wanted to drive him but Matt said no, he'd just take the bus. My mother gave him a St. Christopher medal to wear around his neck and some rosary beads to carry in his pocket. He put the medal on right there in the kitchen for her. The old man focused on the immediate details: When did he leave for San Francisco? When did he head overseas? When would his tour officially begin? When would he have his first R & R?

"Maybe your mother and I will meet you in Hawaii," my father said.

"That would be great, Dad," Matt answered.

Out by the car, the old man said his last words to his oldest son.

"Be careful over there Matt. Be smart."

"I will, Dad, don't worry."

A short while later, after one more cup of coffee, my mother kissed Matt for the last time. Then he and I walked uptown together. The crazy summer was far behind us, distant and faded, like a dream, and the war was up ahead, distant and unknown, like a dream, and there we were in the middle, sitting on a bench, waiting for a bus. I didn't think he was going to die, but he did. That goddamn bus came around the corner and we stood up and shook hands and hugged and we almost cried but we didn't and he got on the bus. He got on the bus and I spoke to him for the last time through the window.

"Hang in there, Matt. Okay?"

"Okay."

"All right."

"You too."

"Okay."

The bus wheezed when the driver put it in gear.

"I love you, brother," Matt said as the bus started to move. It was the one and only time he ever said it. Then the goddamn bus went down the goddamn street, turned the goddamn corner and was gone. I never saw him again. I should have known it was going to be a long season. Now I miss him every day. And I just want to hear his voice once more. And I just want to know: Where'd that caddy go?

ABOUT THE AUTHOR

• •

DAVID NOONAN is the author of *Neuro-*, an exploration of the world of neurological medicine. *Memoirs of a Caddy* is his first novel. He lives in Los Angeles with his wife and sons.

Superb fiction from St. Martin's Paperbacks

OLIVIA AND JAI
Rebecca Ryman
An epic novel of shattered loyalties, forbidden love and dark betrayal set in the splendor of 19th-century India.
_____ 92568-9 $5.99 U.S./$6.99 Can.

FELLOW PASSENGERS
Louis Auchincloss
A gallery of vivid life portraits, masterworks of wealth, love, power and morals—all with the golden Auchincloss touch.
_____ 92391-0 $3.95 U.S./$4.95 Can.

I, JFK
Robert Mayer
Thirty years after his death, America's favorite president writes his memoirs—and they're unlike anything you've read before!
_____ 92340-6 $4.50 U.S./$5.50 Can.

EMMA WHO SAVED MY LIFE
Wilton Barnhardt
Gil Freeman came to the big city in search of a dream. What he found was cheap Chianti, jobs in a bunny suit...and Emma.
_____ 92183-7 $4.95 U.S./$5.95 Can.

Publishers Book and Audio Mailing Service
P.O. Box 120159, Staten Island, NY 10312-0004
Please send me the book(s) I have checked above. I am enclosing $ _____ (please add $1.50 for the first book, and $.50 for each additional book to cover postage and handling. Send check or money order only—no CODs) or charge my VISA, MASTERCARD or AMERICAN EXPRESS card.

Card number _____

Expiration date _____ Signature _____

Name _____

Address _____

City _____ State/Zip_____
Please allow six weeks for delivery. Prices subject to change without notice. Payment in U.S. funds only. New York residents add applicable sales tax.